Honour Found

BY

ROBERT BARRIGER

16 15 14 13 12 11   10 9 8 7 6 5 4 3 2 1

Honour Found
ISBN: 978-160683-189-2

Published by Harrison House, Inc.
P.O. Box 35035
Tulsa, Oklahoma 74153
harrisonhouse.com

CONTENTS

Foreword

Prologue

1 Where Is the Honour? 17

2 Remembering and Honour 29

3 Keeping Remembrance Alive 37

4 Honour Is Weighty 47

5 The Second Mile Principle 61

6 Stolen Honour 75

7 The Other Side of Sacrifice 95

8 Fighting Full-On to the Finish 113

9 Perseverance and Honour 123

10 What's in a Name? 137

11 Facing Off 147

12 How Do We Honour? 163

Endnotes 183

FOREWORD

Robert and Karyn Barriger are among the most genuine, humble, and dedicated people I have had the privilege to minister with over the years.

More than 25 years ago the Barrigers' answered the call as missionaries to Peru with little more than the desire to serve God and a love for people. Their journey has been a demonstration of honouring God through their faith and their tireless, selfless commitment to the lost and disadvantaged in that nation. Their loyalty is without question and their diligence and attention to the truth of the Gospel can be witnessed in all they do.

However, it is clear to me that the message Robert carries on his life has always been for a far greater reach than Peru alone. In fact, his unique experiences and deep insight into God's Word and nature make this book a worthwhile read. Its pages reflect the wealth of wisdom gleaned from a life of service and sacrifice in the pursuit of God.

The subject of honour is at the core and foundation of Christianity. God is a God of honour and all that He is and says in His Word reflects this. God's heart is to honour His people and for them to practise and live in authentic honour with Him and one another.

Honour is a fleeting quality today and the few who live by its code stand well apart from the rest. It is my heartfelt prayer that this book will impart a spirit of honour to all who read it and that it will restore a sense of honour to the Church around the globe. I pray you will be both inspired and challenged.

Brian Houston
Senior Pastor, Hillsong Church.

WHAT OTHERS ARE SAYING

One of the great blessings of my life is my friendship with Pastor Robert Barriger. He has given his life to bringing honour to Jesus Christ, and to those who serve Him. He is a man who practices what he teaches and preaches.

In this book you will discover one of the greatest, but least understood and practiced principles of Scripture -- the principle of honour. As you read, your heart and mind will come alive with hope and encouragement. You will gain new insights into the power and possibilities that are released when we choose to live honourably, and consistently show honour to others. Don't miss this opportunity to take hold of a divine key that will forever change your life!

Dale O'Shields, Senior Pastor
Church of the Redeemer
Gaithersburg, MD
www.church-redeemer.org

Robert has found a key principle that is missing in our culture and in our churches. He uses examples from the Bible and from history to remind us of our need to remember the hero's that have shaped our lives.

Robert's sacrifice as a missionary to Peru and his success as a pastor is a living testimony to this honour principle. This book is a must read that will add value to your life.

Dr. Don Wilson, Pastor
Christ's Church of the Valley

———•◆•———

Robert Barriger is a man whose life has defined the very meaning of honour and this book is the blueprint for learning how to live a God honouring life to those all around us. Displaying honour is not a lost art, and this book proves just how powerful honour can be in living the life God intended for each of us.

Dino Rizzo, Lead Pastor
Healing Place Church

It takes a man of honour to write about the subject of honour in the way Robert Barriger has done in this book.

He has issued a call to our generation, summoning us to understand the respect and the character that pleases God and ennobles those around us.

Robert lives this message and shows us how we can as well. Don't miss the transformation to be found in these pages.

Stephen Mansfield
New York Times Bestselling Author

———◆———

I have known Robert Barriger for over thirty years. The truths in this book are a genuine reflection of the lifestyle of this man of God. He has proven to be an honourable husband, father, and gospel minister. His respect and honour for his leaders and spiritual fathers is exemplary and impeccable. Who better could write such a book as this? Job well done, Robert! *Honour Found*—a "must read."

Mark T. Barclay, Rev., Ph.D.
Preacher of Righteousness

Honour Found is a great resource that provides insight on the principle of honour, and how to practically apply this principle for success with those you lead, as well as those who lead you.

John C. Maxwell,
Best Selling Author and Leadership Expert
and Founder of The John Maxwell Company.

———◆◆———

Those who have seen dishonour are perhaps the best guardians of honour! Robert Barriger is not only a guardian of honour but also a careful restorer of honour to it's rightful place in our lives. As carefully as one might restore a prized piece of antique furniture, he layer by layer restores honour to it's shiny bright patina. From the shelves of scripture to the newspapers of today Robert skillfully reweaves the fabric of honour. The lessons he has taken to heart we should bear in mind that the reputation of those around us might be safe in our hands. Thank you Robert! Not only for your words but for your life that speaks even more eloquently of honour.

Tommy Tenney
God Chasers

PROLOGUE

Honour's a good brooch to wear in a man's hat at all times.

—*Ben Jonson*
Sixteenth century English dramatist and poet

I have been privy to the wishes of a dying man, a mentor and friend, with a great legacy—only to witness others respond that those wishes did not exist because they were not written down. They insisted the man's wishes didn't apply, that although spoken and recorded on a video, they carried no weight or influence. And I asked myself, *Where is the honour?*

Have you ever witnessed anything like this? A lack of respect, dishonour given to someone you felt should receive more than that? Have you ever screamed inside yourself, *Am I the only one who sees this? Don't you see where you are going, what you are doing, where this will end? How wrong this is!*

How do you feel when you witness someone dishonouring another? A young person may act disrespectfully to an elderly person. Children fight over their inheritance while the parents watch helplessly. Someone disrespects their nation's flag and so greatly offends the soldier who fought under it for that person's freedom.

Broken promises. Unfinished missions. Do these people realize what they are doing? Can't they see it? Does anyone else recognize the wrong?

On a number of occasions I have witnessed siblings wishing their parents would die so they could take their home or demanding, "Give me what is owed to me, now!" It is even worse when someone steals an inheritance that rightfully belongs to the children and leaves them with nothing.

What a shame and disgrace when people seek their own desire at the cost of someone else; taking what others have dedicated their lives to build and achieve—taking what they have not earned; mishandling and abusing the inheritance and legacy of another person.

Does this incense you and make you indignant? Angry?

These kinds of actions are on the rise nowadays due to a lack of honour.

Having *honour* means giving "public esteem"; it's "a showing of usually merited respect: recognition."[1] Too many people just don't believe in honour anymore. Look around you and you'll see that for the most part we've lost our honour, which is why this book has been written. The purpose of this message is to bring awareness and a return to the principle of honour. God has principles by which we are to live—honour being among the most prevalent—if we wish to have a full, satisfying and significant life. He makes these principles clear repeatedly in His Word, instructing us to "choose" life or death, blessing or cursing, even going so far as to implore us to "choose life so that you and your descendants may live."[2]

A good father will leave a legacy for his children, to the third and fourth generation.[3] Shortcuts in life will be offered, but don't be deceived by them. Shortcuts will end up leading you into a ditch! Life (and ultimately a legacy) must be built, little by little, line upon line, with trust, patience, longsuffering, diligence, commitment and honour. Yet the ideal of honour has been sadly misplaced and misunderstood.

Honour is a verb, an action word. You can't just say, "I honour" and think that is enough; action is required. In the dictionary, *honour* has a two-fold definition. It is defined as both a noun and a transitive verb. As a noun, *honour* refers to a person, place or thing, such as the guest of honor. As a transitive verb, however, it indicates the transition from one condition to another and is an action; an active thing.

So you could say that to honour someone or something is an action whereby value, esteem or weight is expressed so as to elevate the place, position, worth or condition of the recipient. If there is someone who should be honoured but the honour is not given or acted upon, then *honour* becomes simply an empty word or worthless title. Yet honour is a biblical principle.

The Ten Commandments given to Moses by God were written as a definition of love and honour. Look at the commandment to honour your father and your mother. This is not just referring to a parent's position or role but is an instruction concerning our conduct and actions, that they should bring honour to our parents. We can honour or dishonour our parents (or any other person) with our actions.

In these pages you will find that God's Word is quite specific concerning our need to honour one another both as individuals and as communities. We are to honour those in positions of authority and responsibility over us including parents, teachers, social and local leaders, government representatives, authorities, police and so on. We also are taught in Scripture to honour those who have made great sacrifices for the betterment of others. For instance, this is what we are doing when we participate in the Lord's Supper; we are remembering and placing value on the sacrifice that God's Son, Jesus, made for us.[4] When Jesus said, "Do this in remembrance of Me,"[5] He was instructing us to never forget what He was about to do.

Something else you'll discover in this book is that to dishonour means to take something lightly. When we do not show honour with our actions, it dishonours. If honour is taken lightly— if it is only lip-service or empty words and is lacking in any substance or action—then this is dishonouring. Our parents make great sacrifices for us; soldiers sacrifice their future so we can have freedom in ours. They are worth honouring and should be honoured.

A message on honour wouldn't be complete without covering ways to show honour. You'll find that one way we honour (among all those mentioned) is to remember and show gratitude. Monuments are found in every major city of the world and have been designed for that purpose. A monument is a memorial—a place of remembrance for a person or event of great significance and consequence.

There is significance and consequence to what you honour in life. What do you remember? What do you take lightly? What carries weight with you? What you honour, you feed and it will grow in your life, right or wrong, good or bad. It will carry weight with you. Honouring your parents, for example, brings long life.[6]

So, are you a person of honour? Would you like to be? Whether you already believe in and give honour, or you take lightly what is worthy of honour, my prayer for you is that this book will make you honour bound by helping you to realize what the workings and purpose of honour are, and enabling you to choose well what and who you will honour. When you honour others and treat them with kindness, it is literally as though you are doing the same for God himself.[7]

Chapter 1

WHERE IS THE HONOUR?

"A son honours his father, and a servant his master. If I am a father, where is the honour due me? If I am a master, where is the respect due me?" says the Lord Almighty.

Malachi 1:6

Martin Savidge, a CNN correspondent, was broadcasting live from Iraq. He had been embedded there with the 1st Marine battalion and was talking with four young marines just a few feet from a foxhole. He spoke highly of these men as he related how well they had been taking care to look out for him since the beginning of the war. At that point in the war, the marines had already endured many hardships and Savidge was visibly moved by their camaraderie.

He turned to the four young men with him and told them he'd cleared it with their commander so they could use his video phone to call home. The 19-year-old marine next to him asked if instead, his platoon sergeant could use his call to contact his pregnant wife whom he had not been able to talk to in three months. A stunned Savidge nodded his consent and the marine ran off to get the sergeant. After a few seconds, Savidge regained his composure and turned back to the three remaining marines with him and inquired who would like to call home first. The marine sitting nearest him responded without a moment's hesitation.

"Sir, if it's all the same to you we would like to call the parents of a buddy of ours, Lance Corporal Brian Buesing of Cedar Key, Florida, who was killed on March 23, 2003 near Nasiriyah, to see how they're doing."

At this Savidge totally broke down and was unable to speak. A speechless moment passed, emotion flooding up in him quite noticeably.

Martin Savidge looked into the camera lens and paused a moment. All he could manage to get out before signing off was "Where do they get young men like this?"

When I first read this article, it came to me through an e-mail that went viral to inboxes everywhere. The story is touching as it speaks of selfless soldiers, fighting for our freedoms and way of life and how they acted heroically, looking out for one another. But, sadly, this story never happened. A quick fact check through CNN revealed that the story was only partially true. Lance Corporal Brian Buesing was indeed killed in action in March of 2003. The remaining details about the selfless acts of the other four marines were apparently fabricated.

Still, the story turned up everywhere. Why? Something in us still believes and looks for true heroes. I think this story became ubiquitous because it captures the essence of what we want to believe about people who serve, they can be heroically selfless. The question is still valid, "Where do they get these guys?" Do they really exist still in today's society? Where is the honour?

Believe me, honour is out there. We don't need to make up stories. There are selfless soldiers, servants and people everywhere around us. Selfless. They are not talking about their good deeds or actions, they are busy doing them. There still are everyday people who live by this principle: do what's right. Whatever the cost, whatever the sacrifice, just do what is right.

I believe this story reveals a basic human need - we need heroes. Someone we can look up to; a role model for our children. Someone we can honour. A reproducible model we can identify with and maybe even become.

Honour. It is a concept that both inspires us and emotes us.

What exactly is honour? What qualifies someone as a person of honour? What are the characteristics? How does someone express honour?

You'll find the answers to those questions in this book, but first, how about you—what do you think of when you think of honour? Do you think of a heroic or legendary character from history or a movie, someone like William Wallace, Mother Teresa or maybe a military hero like General George Patton or Audie Murphy (America's most decorated war veteran of World War II)?

How the definition of honour has changed. Nowadays, it seems the word is devoid of meaning and generally overlooked. Yet it was not always like this. In times past, men and women sacrificed life, love, and limbs for the sake of honour. Those who serve with honour in the armed services are trained to this day that honour is a cardinal virtue. After the Vietnam War, however, the concept of honour was devalued. Up until then, most soldiers considered active duty both an honour and a privilege. The greatest honour was to give your life for your country in the field of duty. You were protecting a principle, a way of life, freedom.

A cornerstone of the United States Army is the motto, "Duty, honour and country." Service with honour is the creed and driving motive behind the officers of the United States armed forces. However, at times many of these men and women have felt as though they are one of the last pillars of honour in our country.

What has happened to the honour?

We look to our government officials and in a lot of cases see disrespect for government authorities, a disregard for truth, and at times, dishonour for our service men and women. Too often those who serve their country in the military feel as though they are a lonely watchman upon a wall. So today, where is the honour?

The Creator of heaven and earth asked that very question of His people a few thousand years ago. In Malachi 1:6 He said, "If I am your Father and master, where are the honour and respect I deserve?" The concept of honour is a deeply biblical principle and at the heart of who God is.

The word and principle of honour are found all through Scripture with such commands as to honour our parents, those who teach us, and those who are in authority over us.[1] Many passages instruct us about honour as a quality of character involving honesty, respect and doing what is morally correct. The Bible is explicit about honouring God. First Samuel 2:30 says that God will honour those who honour Him. The Word even tells us that one day Jesus will honour the faithful with a crown.[2] In fact, throughout the Bible, men and women who honoured their leaders were honoured in return. God honours those who give honour.

How different is the model in our present society. We see so many seeking their own promotion in ways that are not honourable. Yet we are called to be set apart;[3] like a military officer, we are to be a bastion of honour in a decaying environment. Before we can do this we must understand just what it is we are defending—the nature of honour.

BIBLICAL LANGUAGE OF HONOUR

For a long time, I wondered about the true meaning of honour. In my mind, the most honourable person who ever lived was Jesus Christ. Certainly, Almighty God is the One most worthy of all honour. Since He has much to say about honour in His Word, let's take a closer look at the biblical meaning of honour to help establish a foundation of understanding.

One important thing to note is that in biblical language honour has a sense of weightiness. Two Hebrew words are used to this end.

Kabod. The Hebrew word *kabod* is a verb or a word that indicates an action or a condition. This word refers to the great physical weight or quality[4] of something and can also have the emphasis of glory, as found in Nahum 2:9, "Take the spoil of silver; take the spoil of gold! For there is no end of the treasure, the glory and wealth of all the precious furnishings."[5]

There are two nuances of *kabod* when it is used in the sense of honour, as in Genesis 45:13 "You must tell my father of all my honour in Egypt, and of all that you have seen. Hurry and bring my father down here."[6]

First, *kabod* can emphasize the position of an individual within the sphere in which he lives, such as "A gracious woman retaineth honour."[7] Second, *kabod* contains the suggestion of nobility or royalty. "When applied to God," one well-known biblical source says, "the word represents a quality corresponding to Him and by which He is recognized."[8]

Kabed. The second Hebrew word for honour used in biblical language—*kabed*—basically means "heavy,"[9] as in Exodus 17:12: "Moses' hands were heavy; and they took a stone, and put it under him, and he sat thereon; and Aaron and Hur stayed up his hands, the one on the one side, and the other on the other side; and his hands were steady until the going down of the sun."[10]

"Heavy" in this verse implies weariness or heavy-laden—Moses' hands were weary from being held up while Israel prevailed in battle.[11]

In Psalm 38:4, which says, "My guilt overwhelms me—it is a burden too heavy to bear," the heaviness is meant as an enduring, ever-present quality or something that lasts. Basically the word is used as an adjective to describe the weight or worthiness of something and often depicts greatness and splendor.

What is there that has weight in the word honour? Why does the Bible connect these two ideas? Sometimes it helps to bring better understanding of an idea by looking at its opposite.

WHERE DO YOU PUT YOUR WEIGHT?

Something opposite to weighty or heavy would be something light. If honour means to apply the due weight or importance to something, then also by way of consequence, to dishonour would be to take that thing lightly or to treat with a lack of respect—to devalue.

In life there are certain things that should not be taken lightly, that should be given the proper weight (later on we'll take a closer look at them).

The Bible tells us to honour those in authority over us, yet how often we deal lightly with things that need weight (honour, glory) in our lives—our parents, our pastors and leaders, or even the officials that God has placed over us in government.

Jesus said in Matthew 22:21 to "render to Caesar the things that are Caesar's." A modern-day example of obeying His command is when a judge enters the courtroom, people stand to show their respect, if not for the individual, then for the office and the authority that person possesses. We give respect to police officers for the same reason. To salute is another example. Saluting the flag is an action that helps us not take lightly the country in which we live. Those serving the United States armed forces salute officers who are of higher rank.

The symbolic meaning of the military salute is one that is lost on many civilians. It is a gesture of good faith, respect and honour. The hand raised to the eyebrow is an emulation of a centuries-old tradition among knights, who upon seeing each other, would raise the right hand and lift the visor of their helmets so that the other could see his face. It also showed that the right hand was open and free of weapons. This was a gesture of respect and goodwill.

A biblical illustration is when the apostle Paul told several churches in his epistles to "greet each other with a holy kiss."[12] While this is certainly a culture-bound example, the core of the message—honour and respect— is not lost in translation.

In this manner, the word *honour* takes its origin from the word *esteem*—to respect, to be considerate. It has to do with recognizing the value of other people and seeing them through the love of God. Honour also encompasses virtues such as dignity, courage, fidelity, integrity, and excellence of character. Where is the honour now?

Remember one of the scriptural examples of honour we saw earlier—the Ten Commandments' mandate to honour our father and our mother?[13] There's another aspect of this command that's crucial to understand because honouring others benefits us as well. According to Paul, this is the first commandment that comes with a promise. He reminded us of it in Ephesians 6:2–3, saying that through honouring our parents, we would have a long, good life.

Let me explain this a little more. This is not like a magical verse - do this and all will be ok. By applying this principal of honour to your life, it does mean that you point your life in the right direction, get the 'train back on the rails' so that your life gets a momentum and progression to it. This principal is much like Joshua 1:8, where Joshua was told, " Study this Book of Instruction continually. Meditate on it day and night so you will be sure to obey everything written in it. Only then will you prosper and succeed in all you do." Once again, God's promise is if we honour the Book, meditate on it, all we do will prosper. The Message Bible actually states, "You will get where you are going." Doing what is right, practicing the honour principle and meditating on His words, gets your life on the right track; it points your life in the right direction. Then when opposition comes with winds of adversity, you will have built your life on the solid foundation of Godly principals and you will stand instead of fall.

Whatever we honour in life, we add life to. The honour principle points us toward a better life, because it is built on God's promises. The Bible has stated that if we honour parents, it adds life to us.

Similarly, if we honour our pastors or spiritual fathers, it too will add life to us.

On August 3, 1983, I stood with my wife and our two small children at the airport gate ready to fly with my family to South America to be a missionary. There was both fear and excitement in my heart. Fear that this was a one way ticket. Excitement for what God would do for us. A small congregation in San Diego, California, had pledged to send us, pray for us, and financially support us. I knew that this was a financial sacrifice for the few families who would give to help our family. My pastors, George and Rita Evans, had the small congregation sing a send-off song as we boarded the plane that would take us to our new home. I made a commitment that day in my heart. My pastors believed in me and the church believed in me enough to sacrifice and send us on our way. I pledged in my heart, and verbally to my pastors, that I would honour their sacrifice and belief in our family, and that I would never intentionally do anything to bring embarrassment to their belief in us and what we were called to do. I would honour them by fulfilling the call I felt God had placed on my life.

That day we left in tears, praying one day we would return, rejoicing. Psalm 126:6 says "They weep as they go to plant their seed, but they sing as they return with the harvest." After 28 years, our ministry in South America has been fruitful. I believe this is largely because of this honour principle. I thank the Lord for a pastor who discipled me, believed in me, and sent me. Though we did go through hard seasons, and even some misunderstandings, I believe my heart to honour my pastor, even in a sense my desire to make him proud of the day he sent our family, has kept my life pointed in the right direction.

Many people live their life giving honour to the wrong things. What they honour, where they put their weight, they also place their life.

What are you investing your life into? What have you chosen to esteem or respect with your heart? Are you honouring and esteeming your Christianity and your heavenly Father, or have you taken them lightly?

When asked what the most important commandment was, Jesus said, "You must love the Lord your God with all your heart, all your soul, and all your mind…. A second is equally important: 'Love your neighbor as yourself.'"[14] Even more so, Jesus commanded us to love each other as He loves us.[15] Love is not without honour. Romans 12:10 says, "Be devoted to one another in brotherly love; honour one another above yourself."[16] Another translation of this passage states that we are to "give preference to one another in honour."[17] This is not empty semantics. The concept of honour cannot be understood without the pre-eminence of preferring others.

Jesus said something else about loving others: that there is no greater love than for someone to lay down his life for his friends[18] — as a soldier will lay down his life for his comrade and for his country, that sacrifice is never to be held lightly. Jesus illustrated this greatest expression of love when He went to the cross in our place. To take

His sacrifice lightly is to dishonour Him. In honouring His sacrifice, life is added through honour.

Honouring others takes a certain act on our part, one that as we'll see next, is a primary source of honour.

Chapter 2

REMEMBERING AND HONOUR

I remember the days of old. I ponder all your great works and think about what you have done.

Psalm 143:5

Van T. Barfoot believes that we must never forget our heroes. The flag, a symbol of the nation he fought for in WWII, has a deep, profound (heavy) meaning for the 92-year-old. A retired colonel, veteran of three wars (World War II, Korea and Vietnam), and Congressional Medal of Honor and Purple Heart recipient, it is said that he has raised the flag flying high in front of his house at sunrise and lowered it at sunset ever since serving in the U.S. Army. What an obvious act of remembrance and honour for the sacrifices and high price paid by thousands of war heroes for our freedom.

Unfortunately, how soon many of us forget. Some of Van's neighbors didn't want him to fly the flag on the flagpole in his front yard. Seems it was a matter of decorum. But Barfoot refused to take it down and faced court action.

Perhaps the opposition didn't know about or remember Van's heroics during his enlistment. In one day during World War II, for instance, he single-handedly destroyed two German machine gun nests, killed eight enemy soldiers and took 17 prisoners, and faced a tank head-on before destroying it and killing the crew—and he wasn't about to back down now. Through the pressure of the press and his tenacity, his flag now flies proudly over his house in honour and remembrance of his country and those who suffered and died for its freedom.[1]

The act of remembering ignites honour. It is even scriptural. Interestingly, in Scripture remembering is often connected with a covenant. When God makes a promise, it is not made lightly. When He enters into covenant, it's His word of honour, so whatever He says is a certainty. The first time *covenant* is mentioned in the Bible is in the book of Genesis, when God sent the Great Flood to the earth. After the Flood, He promised: "As long as the earth remains, there will be planting and harvest, cold and heat, summer and winter, day and night."[2]

In other words, as long as the earth endures these are certainties we can rely upon. God had destroyed all life on the earth with a worldwide flood because man had moved so far from Him since Adam and Eve disobeyed Him in the Garden and brought sin into the world.[3] However, He saved a single family—the family of Noah—by instructing him to build an ark.

When the floodwaters receded, God gave Noah and his family the go-ahead to leave the ark and release all the animals. Once that was accomplished, Noah built an altar and offered a sacrifice to God that pleased Him. Then God made another covenant with Noah and, ultimately, all mankind, saying,

> "I will remember my covenant with you and with all living creatures. Never again will the floodwaters destroy all life. When I see the rainbow in the clouds, I will remember the eternal covenant between God and every living creature on earth." Then God said to Noah, "Yes, this rainbow is the sign of the covenant I am confirming with all the creatures on earth."[4]

God gave the promise that never again would He flood the earth and He gave the rainbow as a sign or seal to remind Him and all creatures of this.

The Bible consistently talks about things God remembers— things that we should remember too.

EAT IT ALL!

One biblical instance of something God wants us to remember is found in Exodus 12 and 13, which talk about the plague of the firstborns. Before God allowed this plague, He gave specific instructions to Moses and Aaron concerning Israel.

> Announce to the whole community of Israel that on the tenth day of this month each family must choose a lamb or a young goat for a sacrifice, one animal for each household. If a family is too small to eat a whole animal, let them share

with another family in the neighborhood. Divide the animal according to the size of each family and how much they can eat. The animal you select must be a one-year-old male, either a sheep or a goat, with no defects.

Take special care of this chosen animal until the evening of the fourteenth day of this first month. Then the whole assembly of the community of Israel must slaughter their lamb or young goat at twilight. They are to take some of the blood and smear it on the sides and top of the door frames of the houses where they eat the animal. That same night they must roast the meat over a fire and eat it along with bitter salad greens and bread made without yeast. Do not eat any of the meat raw or boiled in water. *The whole animal*—including the head, legs, and internal organs—must be roasted over a fire. Do not leave any of it until the next morning.[5]

A particular part of this passage that stands out is verse 9 because it commands the whole animal to be roasted and eaten, with nothing left out. Here the Bible says that each Hebrew family had to eat the entire lamb—all of it. Personally, there are certain parts of a lamb that I like to eat: the ribs, chops, and steaks, among others. However, some lamb parts are just not appealing to the palate, let alone to look at...like the offal! Yet God instructed His people specifically to eat it all and not to leave any of it. They had to eat the lot.

This detail is important for a couple of reasons. First, the whole lamb is a reflection of Jesus Christ, the sacrificial Lamb upon whom

God placed the sin of the world.[6] Once we invite Jesus into our hearts and receive Him as our Lord and Savior, we should begin to embrace all the "parts" that entail living as a Christian.

We enjoy, even love, certain parts of the Christian life—forgiveness (being forgiven!), grace, peace, healing and love, to name only a few. Some parts, however, we don't enjoy or don't like to "eat"—sacrifice, obedience, offering, and forgiving our enemy, among others. Certain portions of the Gospel just aren't so easy to eat. Yet the Word of God says to eat *all* of the Lamb. So, whichever way we look at it, we don't have the luxury of selective remembering, of picking and choosing which pieces of Scripture we'll accept; it's all or none. We are to receive *all* that the Bible says concerning Jesus.

After God told the Israelites to eat "the whole lamb," He went on to make a promise to Moses and Aaron concerning the blood of each slain lamb (sacrificed by every Jewish household) that pertains to us as well.

> The blood on your doorposts will serve as a sign, marking the houses where you are staying. When I see the blood, I will pass over you. This plague of death will not touch you when I strike the land of Egypt.[7]

Spiritually speaking, when the blood of Jesus is on the door of our hearts through salvation, death cannot enter—we have eternal life. The angel of death (the enemy, satan) must pass over us. Here's what that means, in the Old Testament, the lamb's blood was applied to the doorpost of each Hebrew home, and when the death angel saw the sacrificial blood, he passed by that house. In the New Testament, Jesus is called the Lamb of God. When we become a Christian, we do so by giving Jesus control of our lives and asking Him to forgive us of our sins (the things we have all done that offend both God and others).[8] At that time Jesus, God's Lamb, becomes our substitute,[9] the sacrificial Lamb, and His blood is now applied to the doorpost of our hearts. This happens by faith—by believing in Him, that He paid the full price for all of our sins—and by asking Him into our hearts, our lives. God sees the blood of His Son over our lives, He sees that His Son paid the price for our sins, that He took our wrong, and made it right, and we are forgiven.[10]

The blood in the first Passover was real, the death angel saw it, honoured it, and passed over it. Today, Jesus' blood is real as well. He paid the price in full, God sees His Son's blood over our lives, God honours it, and death has lost its sting, meaning that we are given eternal life.

Let's look at Exodus 13 which tells why this is important .

NEVER FORGET

Then the Lord said to Moses, "Dedicate to me every firstborn among the Israelites. The first offspring to be born, of both humans and animals, belongs to me."

So Moses said to the people, *"This is a day to remember forever*—the day you left Egypt, the place of your slavery. Today the Lord has brought you out by the power of his mighty hand. (Remember, eat no food containing yeast.) On this day in early spring, in the month of Abib, you have been set free. You must celebrate this event in this month each year after the Lord brings you into the land of the Canaanites, Hittites, Amorites, Hivites, and Jebusites. (He swore to your ancestors that he would give you this land—a land flowing with milk and honey.)[11]

This passage is talking about the Feast of Passover, a time when Israel was called to remember their deliverance from slavery. It was to be celebrated each year since that time in Egypt and it has continued to be celebrated by Jewish people even today. In fact, the celebration of Passover took place just before the crucifixion of Jesus Christ and the two events have been entwined from that time forward. The Greek word *Pascha*, originally meaning Passover, came to mean Easter as well.[12]

Every year as we celebrate Easter and are remembering the crucifixion of Jesus, the Jews are remembering the Passover: *"Never forget what I have done for you."*[13] In the Old Testament, God commanded them to remember their deliverance. In the New Testament, just before Jesus went to the cross He told His disciples, "This is my body, which is given for you. *Do this to remember me.*"[14]

Are you beginning to see the theme? God is imploring His people to remember and never forget what He has done. In this case, He wants us to never forget the sacrifice that Jesus made on our behalf and to comprehend the immeasurable value of this event because of its eternal impact on mankind.

God isn't unreasonable or demanding about our remembering His goodness in our lives; He knows the benefits we can receive. The problem is it's all too easy to forget.

It is true that when life gets tough, when we face challenges, sickness, betrayal or whatever it may be, it is not necessarily an easy or natural thing to remember God's promises at such times. For that reason, He has established milestones or memorials such as the Communion or the Lord's Supper, and Easter or the passion of the Christ, among others, to help us.

Chapter 3

KEEPING REMEMBRANCE ALIVE

Bless the LORD, O my soul, and forget not all his benefits.

Psalm 103:2 KJV

In Peru, where I presently live, we celebrate our independence as a special day. On this day Peru's people remember that once their descendants served under another nation but today they enjoy their national freedom. So each year we celebrate by gathering in our homes over a special meal recalling how it was before and how it is now. Although the fight for freedom was neither ours nor our fathers' battle, it is a significant part of our history and our heritage. In remembering, we remain thankful and appreciative of what we now take for granted—we attribute the due "weight" or value to this day. What would happen to us as a nation if we forgot?

What happens to us when we forget what God has done for us?

A lot is spoken of in the Bible concerning things to remember and what happens when we forget.

Here is a very sad passage from Hosea 2:8 and 13:6 that talks about someone who forgot God's goodness.

> She doesn't realize it was I who gave her everything she has—the grain, the new wine, the olive oil; I even gave her silver and gold. But she gave all my gifts to Baal.

> But when you had eaten and were satisfied, you became proud and forgot me.

Each time God does something significant for us, we should treat it with weight by remembering it in some way. How many times has God healed us or someone dear to us? What about all the times He provided for our needs when we couldn't and He delivered us from danger or loss? As in this passage from Hosea, it is all too easy to forget the goodness of God to us. In forgetting, however, we can become a prey to our enemy.[1]

In Deuteronomy 25:17–19, we read these strong words on forgetting:

> *Never forget* what the Amalekites did to you as you came from Egypt. They attacked you when you were exhausted and weary, and they struck down those who were straggling behind. They had no fear of God. Therefore, when the Lord your God has given you rest from all your enemies in the land he is giving you as a special possession, you must destroy the Amalekites and erase their memory from under heaven. *Never forget this!*

God was warning Israel in this passage to never forget how their enemy, Amalek and the Amalekites, attacked them. Amalek's M.O. was to attack from behind when the people were tired and weakened. Isn't this a tactic the enemy, satan, uses with us even today? He'll strike at a weak moment when our guard may be down or we are already suffering and our strength is failing us.[2] He goes for those who are weak in some way whether physically, emotionally or spiritually. His motive is simple—to make us forget what God has done for us. *Satan knows that to forget puts distance between us and God.*

There is a saying, gratitude confirms relationships. So when we remember all God has done for us and are thankful, we draw closer to Him. A heart that is forgetful is distant. Something else is occupying that space, something else has our attention. Often what occupies our attention is the very blessing He blessed us with. Wealth can be a great blessing when it is a tool to be used for good, but as we just read in Hosea, God blessed them, and they forgot. They actually served other gods using His blessing. The distance is therefore on man's end, not God's.

As we remember God's benefits, as we draw close to Him, He is always there to draw closer to us.[3] King David (who was also a psalmist) wrote about drawing close to God often in the Psalms, but one particular time he said that in God's presence is "the pathway" of our lives, "fullness of joy," and "pleasures forevermore"![4]

So how do we remember God's benefits to us, the important things He has done for us in our personal lives?

I once heard about a man named George Muller who recorded all of his prayers in a book and marked the dates by those that were answered. After he died, this book was discovered and it revealed over 50,000 answered prayers in George's life. How incredibly profound, and what a testimony to the faithfulness of God! Think what would have been lost and thus forgotten for future generations had George not taken the time so diligently and tirelessly to honour and remember the work of God in his life.

That book of answered prayer became a powerful memorial to God.

A STAKE TO REMEMBER

I remember hearing about a farmer who had heard that salvation was by grace. He received his salvation, but the voice of the enemy came to condemn him in such a way that every time the farmer remembered his mistakes he would feel as though he wasn't saved. So whenever he sinned, he felt that there was no forgiveness for him. This was his great struggle—until one day he got down on his knees and prayed, "Lord, I receive You in my heart once and forever. By Your grace I am saved. I receive Your grace."

Thereupon he took a wooden stake and marking the date upon it, drove it firmly into the ground near his shed. Sure enough, that following week the voice of condemnation returned, but this time the farmer said, "No Satan, I have already been forgiven for my mistakes," and he ran to his stake by the shed to remember what he had done. He had made a memorial to his salvation…to remember. That is actually one translation of the word *memorial* in Scripture.

The Hebrew word for *memorial* can be translated as "remembrance" or "scent" (we'll discuss the latter in a moment). the Greek word for it can be translated as a "reminder" or "record."[5] A modern-day definition of *memorial* is "something that keeps remembrance alive."[6] Let's look at two types of memorials that give honour through remembering.

A MEMORIAL TO GOD

In the Old Testament, God told Joshua to erect a memorial for the specific purpose of remembrance when He opened up the Jordan River so the Israelites could cross over to the Promised Land.

> When all the people had crossed the Jordan, the LORD said to Joshua, "Now choose twelve men, one from each tribe. Tell them, 'Take twelve stones from the very place where the priests are standing in the middle of the Jordan. Carry them out and pile them up at the place where you will camp tonight.'"

Joshua did as God instructed him and told the twelve men:

> "We will use these stones to build a memorial. In the future your children will ask you, 'What do these stones mean?' Then you can tell them, 'They remind us that the Jordan River stopped flowing when the Ark of the Lord's Covenant

went across.' These stones will stand as a memorial among the people of Israel forever."

So the men did as Joshua had commanded them. They took twelve stones from the middle of the Jordan River, one for each tribe, just as the LORD had told Joshua. They carried them to the place where they camped for the night and constructed the memorial there.

Joshua also set up another pile of twelve stones in the middle of the Jordan, at the place where the priests who carried the Ark of the Covenant were standing. And they are there to this day.[7]

This passage from Joshua 4 reveals God's heart toward His people and that He understands our humanity and its struggles and weaknesses; He knows that we forget. We've seen that He instructs us to be very intentional about remembering His hand at work in our lives—but not only for our sakes. *It is also for the generations that are to come.*

God is very solemn and intentional about this because of the power of honour in our lives and in the generations after us. What is the power of honour? It is simply our reward for doing what is right, for living an honourable life. It is said that if we fail to learn from history, we are destined to repeat it. I believe that history does not actually repeat itself; rather man just makes the same mistakes over and over again so the consequences are repeated. So for a parent to sit with their children to explain the significance of a memorial is to ensure the lesson is carried on through the generations and guard against repeating the mistakes of the past. Honour remembers the past to point us forward. In forgetting the past, we risk repeating its mistakes.

Some memorials are lessons for all to see. In Israel today, there is a memorial to the victims of the Holocaust. The Holocaust museum is a sobering reminder of a past sin that should never be forgotten and never repeated. As you walk through the museum you see reminders of the train rides, the concentration camps; pieces of clothing, a sandal, a yellow star. At the end of the museum's historical narrative is the Hall of Names — a repository for the Pages of Testimony of millions of Holocaust victims, a memorial to many who are anonymous no longer. The Hall of Names is a reminder to remember these real people who were caught in an horrific injustice because of their faith. See their name, see their suffering and see their sacrifice. Learn and move forward – don't go back to the errors of our predecessors.

Making a record and giving weight to that memory, points us forward. It recognizes and adds value to the past for our children when they encounter such a memorial. It gives us an opportunity to teach them that history does not need to repeat itself. To honour is to remember and to teach the next generation that we have made our mistakes; let's learn from them and not repeat them - now let's move forward.

A MEMORIAL OF PRAYER

King David talked about a memorial of prayer in Psalm 141:2 when he said to God, "Accept my prayer as incense offered to you."

In the book of Revelation, John's vision of heaven included his witnessing the fullfillment of this truth when he saw Jesus, "the Lion of the tribe of Judah,"[8] and "Lamb of God,"[9] step forward to open the scroll.

> As he took the scroll, the four living beings and the twenty-four elders fell down before the Lamb. Each one had a harp, *and they held gold bowls filled with incense—the prayers of God's people!*[10]

The King James Version describes the incense in this verse as "golden vials full of odours [or aromas]."

> Then [an] angel with a gold incense burner came and stood at the altar. And a great quantity of incense was given to him to mix with the prayers of God's people, to be offered on the gold altar before the throne.[11]

The idea here is that our prayers hold so much weight with God that they ascend before His throne as a pleasant fragrance and are accepted by Him.

HEARD AND PRESERVED

An especially poignant story that illustrates the bigger picture to us as individuals is found in Acts 10.

> There was a certain man in Caesarea called Cornelius, a centurion of the band called the Italian band, a devout man, and one who feared God with all his house, who gave many

alms to the people and prayed to God always. He saw in a vision clearly, about the ninth hour of the day, an angel of God coming in to him and saying unto him, "Cornelius!" And when he looked on him, he was afraid and said, "What is it, lord?" And he said unto him, "Thy prayers and thine alms have risen up as a memorial before God."[12]

Cornelius, a God-fearing man and a soldier (a Roman captain of 100 men), lived his life in such a way before God and man that he not only caught the attention of heaven but became the very first non-Jew to convert to Christianity. Peter was in Joppa, a city some distance south of Caesarea where Cornelius lived, when he heard God speak to him about this centurion. God prepared Peter to receive Cornelius' messengers when they arrived and to journey with them to Cornelius' home. There Peter freely preached the gospel of Jesus Christ to him whereupon both Cornelius and his entire household were saved.

What does all this mean for us today? Our prayers, generosity and kindness to others are both heard and preserved by God. God remembers them (as He did those of Cornelius). Our offerings, the sacrifices we make for love and devotion to God and His Church, our kindness to others—these things are always before Him. That is absolutely mind-blowing when you really think about it! Nothing we do in His name is lost to Him. And not only that, God can answer our prayers at any place, in any way, always—when we lift our offering and prayers to Him.

God gives weight to our prayers, and in honouring them, He honours us.[13] How much more should we show Him the honour He is due?

Chapter 4

HONOUR IS WEIGHTY

Nothing is more honourable than a grateful heart.
—Seneca
First century Roman philosopher

I have taken several trips to Arlington National Cemetery in Washington, DC. Most of the American heroes are buried there. It is a very moving place. A particular part of this cemetery impacts me immensely—the Tomb of the Unknown Soldier. It is an awe-inspiring memorial.

Within this tomb lie three American soldiers.[1] Of these three soldiers one was killed in World War I, the second in World War II and the third gave his life in the Korean War. The inscription on the tomb reads:

"Here rests in honoured glory an American soldier known but to God."

What gives this memorial tomb such added impact is the special guard of honour who stand vigil over it. For 24 hours a day, 7 days a week, 365 days a year since 1937 a soldier from the Old Guard, the 3rd U.S. Infantry Regiment, keeps watch. The soldier on this duty "marches along a 63-foot walkway in exactly 21 paces, before turning to face the tomb for exactly 21 seconds, turning to face the opposite direction for another 21 seconds, and then retracing his steps to repeat the process. Each turn the guard makes is precise and is instantly followed by a loud click of the heels as he snaps them together."[2] No matter the weather—rain, hail, snow or sunshine— they carry out their sacred duty.

These men are called the Tomb Sentinels. Only the most elite soldiers are permitted to perform this consecrated duty as they march continually before the tomb. The vigil has been performed strictly and religiously by every soldier on that duty, day and night, without exception, for over seventy years (at the writing this book).

The intense respect shown for these unknown soldiers is deeply moving and humbling. The Old Guard follow a rigid and vehemently protected protocol even in their preparation for duty for three soldiers unknown to them or any man, only to God.

"The sentinels spend four to six hours each day just shining their shoes between guard walks. 'That's one pair of shoes,' [Spc. John] Tilley says. 'To get a brand-new pair of shoes ready to go takes about 40 to 50 hours.'

"New shoes are sanded down to eliminate their texture and then re-shined. A power sander is used to sand down the soles of the shoes, which also are shined again.

"'We shine, shine, shine and sand down the shine, get all the texture out and start shining them back up,' Tilley says. 'It's just a long, long process.'"[3]

A number of years ago, a hurricane was heading toward Arlington National Cemetery. The commanding officer of the Sentinels gave permission to "stand down." It was the first time in over 70 years that this order was given—to take cover if it became dangerous. Here's one newspaper's description of the situation:

> "During winds that turned over vehicles and turned debris into projectiles, the measured step continued. One fellow said, 'I've got buddies getting shot at in Iraq who would kick my [backside] if word got to them that we let them down. I sure…have no intention of spending my Army career being known as the…idiot who couldn't stand a little light breeze and shirked his duty.'

> "On the ABC evening news, it was reported recently that, because of the dangers from Hurricane Isabel approaching Washington, DC, the military members assigned the duty of guarding the Tomb of the Unknown Soldier were given permission to suspend the assignment. They refused. 'No way, Sir!'

> "Soaked to the skin, marching in the pelting rain of a tropical storm, they said that guarding the Tomb was not just an assignment; it was the highest honour that can be afforded to a service person."[4]

The hurricane came and went and the following morning the soldiers were found still keeping their post; they had continued their guard throughout the storm. Trees had fallen and conditions were perilous and when one of the soldiers was later asked wasn't it dangerous, the reply came, "Yes." When asked why they had continued, he essentially answered, " my debt to duty is not part-time." Honour is weighty. These men did not take their duty lightly.

How sad but true that many Christians do not honour or give due weight or value to their faith or their calling—they take it lightly. Our walk with God is not part-time. Jesus didn't come to earth, die and then be raised to eternal life with a part-time attitude. Not possible! Calvary would never have taken place and our salvation would not have been purchased if that was the approach He took.

The apostle Paul put it perfectly: "For to me, to live is Christ and to die is gain."[5] There's nothing part-time about that! For Jesus, it was honour and duty before personal cost, "Saying, Father, if thou be willing, remove this cup from me: nevertheless not my will, but thine, be done."[6] And I know that I am indescribably grateful for that. We must never devalue the work of the cross of Christ by treating it as common, ordinary or even incidental—of less importance than other things in our lives.

Jesus made this statement at the Last Supper: "This is my body which is given for you: this do in remembrance of me."[7] We've talked about that verse already, but it bears mentioning again to stress that we must never forget. Sometimes never forgetting what God has done for us can stretch our faith when we find ourselves in some kind of battle. The apostle Paul called it "the good fight of faith."[8]

FIGHT THE GOOD FIGHT

Often the battles we face are many and incredibly challenging, but we were never promised that faith in Christ would be easy. By definition, *faith* means risk; it means that there will be unanswered questions—otherwise, why would we need faith? Of course it won't always be easy and that's exactly why it's of such vital importance that we never forget the price that was paid for our salvation.[9]

My wife amazes me. She is fighting cancer in her body and the fight is costly to her and to our family. But every morning as I walk into our bathroom I see the walls filled with notes containing scripture verses of healing. She refuses to forget the promises of God concerning her battle. Her commitment and her faith are not part-time. Her ministry is not part-time; it is her way of life. People like her remove our excuses. Will we continue with our Christian vigilance even when it isn't convenient? When it is difficult and costing us? When it means sacrifice?

The sentinels of the Tomb of the Unknown Soldier, despite personal hardship and risk, did not look for an excuse to quit, but continued on their guard 24 hours a day, 7 days a week, and faithfully kept the shoe-shining regimen—all in honour of three dead soldiers who sacrificed their futures in order that we might have one. Nobody even knows their names, except God. Yet those three men were very real people with lives of their own, with a story and a past.

They had parents who would have been both proud of them for their decision to defend their country and at the same time fearful for their lives and what they would face. Those three men left behind loved ones, prayers for their safety, plans for the future, sweethearts or wives…they would return, unknown. Their parents would have watched, anxiously awaiting news of their return, all in vain. Their sons had fallen in battle and their connection and identity to them was lost forever.

Would we fight the battle of faith if nobody ever knew; if we were unknown? Sometimes the fight is made easier because of the desire for or promise of recognition, or at the very least to be remembered. But would you and I continue to fight to hold onto our faith if no one knew what we were doing or what we were going through?

We may be unknown to others, but God speaks over us (as I believe He did those unknown soldiers), "These are Mine"— unknown to the world but known intimately by Him.

Last night, a group of people I'm not familiar with stayed behind after the service and cleaned our church. I don't know their identity, but God does. He saw them. Sometimes nobody sees the good and noble things we do. Some of these things are not for the eyes of others, but for His eyes alone. Some do good deeds because of who they think is watching them; others sacrifice in secret, only for His eyes, for the honour of God—an offering, act of service or kindness unseen. Are we as Christians willing to live like that?

FULFILLING THE CALL

Exodus 31 gives an account of a man who was willing to do his best for God's eyes only, which meant living behind the scenes to fulfill God's call on his life. The story is about Moses coming down from Mount Sinai with the freshly inscribed Ten Commandments of God—the tablets of the Law. In several earlier chapters of Exodus, God had given Moses instructions on how to build the tabernacle. This chapter begins with God instructing him on who would "make the sacred tent and its furnishings."[10]

> "Look, I have specifically chosen Bezalel son of Uri, grandson of Hur, of the tribe of Judah. I have filled him with the Spirit of God, giving him great wisdom, ability, and expertise in all kinds of crafts. He is a master craftsman, expert in working with gold, silver, and bronze. He is skilled in engraving and mounting gemstones and in carving wood. He is a master at every craft!"[11]

Bezalel was evidently an artisan with extraordinary talent and an absolute master of making lifelike images. As Moses began to declare the commandments of the Law to his people, Bezalel would have been among them all, listening, processing, considering, adjusting as the second commandment was read out:

> "You must not make for yourself an idol of any kind or an image of anything in the heavens or on the earth or in the sea.

You must not bow down to them or worship them, for I, the LORD your God, am a jealous God who will not tolerate your affection for any other gods. I lay the sins of the parents upon their children; the entire family is affected—even children in the third and fourth generations of those who reject me. But I lavish unfailing love for a thousand generations on those who love me and obey my commands."[12]

What must Bezalel have thought when he heard this? As a master artisan of images, surely it would have confronted him. Perhaps his thoughts were something along the lines of "No! How can this be? That is my life's work! How can this work for me?"

Imagine the impact these words must have had on Bezalel! He was faced with the reality that he would never again be able to craft another image of the type he had been crafting. What's more, his most masterful work containing an image would now never be seen by a human other than one priest, the High Priest, who was allowed to enter the inner sanctuary of the Tabernacle once a year to offer a blood sacrifice and burn incense for the atonement of the sins of the Hebrew people.[13] All that Bezalel crafted for the Tabernacle was only for the Holy of Holies—to be always concealed behind a thick veil.

Artists take great satisfaction and fulfillment from others' appreciation of their work. Bezalel made the solid gold angels who covered the ark, but in essence God was saying, "This is for My eyes alone and I will hide it in the Holy place." Only one priest with the fear of God would ever see it—no other, only God. Would you or I create a masterpiece if God were the only One who was ever going to enjoy it?

Some time ago, my friend Pastor Dino Rizzo, shared a story from Ecclesiastes with me that also tells of a man whose effort went unnoticed by all, but God:

"Here is another bit of wisdom that has impressed me as I have watched the way our world works. There was a small town with only a few people, and a great king came with his army and besieged it. A poor, wise man knew how to save the town, and so it was rescued. But afterward no one thought to thank him."[14]

This is curious—a poor unidentified man's wisdom saved his small town. Yet he was never thanked and, in fact, he was promptly forgotten. His story even has only two verses in the Bible. His people forgot him, but God did not.

What does this have to do with us? *Would we still do something for somebody if no one knew about it?* When we look to do something without thought of return, I believe that God sees, He remembers and He is glorified.

In our church we take part in an annual event known as "Servolution." As a church we go out into our community and perform acts of kindness and generosity without thought of return. I love this time, especially for what it builds into the lives of our people and our community. Sometimes people recognize what we do, but the most impact is made when, like the sentinels of the Tomb of the Unknown Soldier, honour is given to someone unknown.

It is my desire to give due honour to those unseen and unknown who serve in our churches; those who stay behind to clean after everyone else has gone home, those who watch over our cars in the parking lot while we are enjoying the service, those who rise early to rehearse many extra hours so that we can enjoy beautiful worship music without distraction. So many give of themselves in a selfless way to make church so wonderful. Although they may go unrecognized by man, they are recognized by God.

Pastors are another group who do so much for others but often aren't recognized by man (they always are by God). The Bible, however, is quite clear about people honouring leadership, specifically in the church.

THE WEIGHT OF DOUBLE HONOUR

Elders who do their work well should be respected and should be paid well [or "worthy of double honour"[15]], especially those who work hard at both preaching and teaching. For the Scripture says…"Those who work deserve their pay!"[16]

The word *elders* here refers to those who preside over churches. The primary function of elders is to lead their church well. When this passage speaks of "double honour", double refers to two types of honour: (1) respect for ruling well and (2) adequate pay for their diligent care of the church (1 Cor. 9:1–14). Elders who preach and teach the scriptures are worthy of this double honour.

The Greek root from the term *double honour* (used in the *New King James* version of the opening scripture) literally means "value" or "valuable"[17]; in other words, "let them be counted worthy of double value." In the context of this passage, Paul was addressing administrative issues—administrating the widows and various areas of the daily running of the church. He was making the point here that those who administrate the church are worthy of honour, and if they administrate the church well, they are worthy of double honour.

God is concerned with taking care of His people. A common attitude is that the pastor should be just one of the people, but that's definitely not how God sees it. Many who have oversight concerning the things of God receive their living accordingly. Those who excel and are considered by God to be worthy of honour, their merit is directly related to their excellence in ministry and administration. So it would be fair to say that the manner in which these things are conducted is of clear importance.

This is also highlighted by Jesus in the Parable of the Talents. Those who administrated the talents well were honoured: "Well done, my good and faithful servant."[19] However, to the one who buried his talent in the ground came dishonour, brought upon by his laziness and irresponsibility. When we take what God has given us and are faithful to work and develop it, this brings honour to us and to Him.

The same exhortation is found in 1 Thessalonians 5:12–13 where Paul makes this plea:

"Dear brothers and sisters, honour those who are your leaders in the Lord's work. They work hard among you and give you spiritual guidance. Show them great respect and wholehearted love because of their work. And live peacefully with each other."

Why is this seemingly such a critical issue? We live in a world that not only lacks respect for authority, but in many cases publicly ridicules both the pastor and his ministry. A pastor is constantly forced to deal with the demands and pressures of ministry and the church. In 2 Corinthians 12:7, Paul talked about this firsthand—it could be argued that the "thorn in the flesh" he refers to is actually his constant concern for the church. The pressures a pastor is subjected to are often extremely intense; it is quite possible that the reason many people don't honour their pastor is simply because they don't know that they should.

A lot of pastors are uncomfortable about preaching or teaching the need for honour from their pulpit and it's not difficult to understand why. What do you think would happen in the majority of churches if the pastor announced his message was from 1 Timothy 5:17, where it says he is worthy of double honour? It's probably safe to assume that most would leave the church that day declaring the pastor an egotist, proud or self-seeking and in need of a lesson on humility! It is obvious why this is not a subject publicly discussed by pastors themselves because it is such a "hot potato." Nevertheless, uncomfortable as it is, the Bible admonishes us to take care of our pastors in this manner.

You can almost feel Paul's heart. It's like he's saying, "Recognize and value the work pastors do among you." Pastors have the weighty responsibility of the spiritual care of the church and will be judged accordingly.[20]

Think about the implications if all the people in every local church got behind their pastors to honour and acknowledge them by saying, "Pastor, we are with you, we stand with you together for the vision that God has called you to for our city." Such encouragement and declaration of unity would have an incredibly positive impact.

In a recent survey on clergy statistics, roughly 80 percent of pastors think about resigning the church because they don't feel appreciated.[21] Apparently a pastor will experience, on average, one or two betrayals of some form every month of the year. Psychologists say that it can take as long as a year or even two to overcome a single betrayal. Do the math. Pastors have to deal with the threat of discouragement and depression on a compounding and daily basis.

It is true that God has called pastors to shepherd and bring together His body,[22] but if we fail to value and support our pastors, the cost is extremely high. The Word of God says that if you "smite the shepherd, the sheep...shall be scattered."[23] Satan relies on this principle and knows it well—he targets pastors and their families, but if people would stand together with and honour their pastor, the anointing, power and blessing that would be poured out on all would be phenomenal. The fact is, according to Scripture, honouring our pastors is a part of serving the Lord.

Here's the bottom line: to be a true servant of Christ is to serve Him with your whole life. Jesus' sacrifice was not part-time or convenient. Ask yourself, *Would I do this if no one else knew?* Declare it now by faith:

> "I am a Christian full time—in the storm and in the sunshine, in the darkness and in the light, in the scorching sun and in the freezing cold, I continue my watch. I do not take lightly what God has done for me and what others have done for me."

The lesson is simple—as Christians our lives are to be established and built upon the principle of the "second-mile."

Chapter 5

THE SECOND MILE PRINCIPLE

No person was ever honoured for what he received. Honour has been the reward for what he gave.

—Calvin Coolidge

I ask myself why? God has done everything for us including the sacrifice of His only Son and yet Jesus himself says He will honour us before the Father...what can we possibly do? All that we do must be by His grace,

Not because of works [not the fulfillment of the Law's demands], lest any man should boast. [It is not the result of what anyone can possibly do, so no one can pride himself in it or take glory to himself.][1]

Nevertheless it is written in God's Word that Jesus himself will one day reward us for our works on earth. This is difficult to comprehend and yet in Matthew 6:17, we are told that what we do privately to help others, God will reward us for openly and in public.

The highest honour the United States Government can bestow is the Congressional Medal of Honor. This medal is only awarded to those who go above and beyond the call of duty; it is only given to members of the military (however, there is a civilian equivalent[2]). Never more than three people in a given year receive this medal. The recipients are soldiers who have acted heroically, extraordinarily above and beyond their call of duty.

While reading about some of these brave men, I discovered something quite fascinating and compelling: they never felt they were deserving of the honour they were given. Instead, their attitude tended to be that what they did was not so much for their country; they did what they felt they had to do for their "brothers"—their fellow soldiers and friends.

One of the citations I came across that stood out to me was of a particular soldier named Sergeant Roy P. Benavidez, who found himself in a battle in the Vietnam War. According to the citation, he "distinguished himself by... fearless personal leadership, tenacious devotion to duty, and extremely valorous actions in the face of overwhelming odds." Here are some excerpts describing his heroic performance:

> On the morning of 2 May 1968, a 12-man Special Forces Reconnaissance Team was inserted by helicopters in a dense jungle area west of Loc Ninh, Vietnam to gather intelligence information about confirmed large-scale enemy activity... on the ground, the team met heavy enemy resistance, and

requested emergency extraction. Three helicopters attempted extraction, but were unable to land due to intense enemy small arms and anti-aircraft fire.

Sergeant Benavidez was at the Forward Operating Base in Loc Ninh monitoring the operation by radio when these helicopters returned to off-load wounded crewmembers and to assess aircraft damage. [He] voluntarily boarded a returning aircraft to assist in another extraction attempt. Realizing that all the team members were either dead or wounded and unable to move to the pickup zone, he directed the aircraft to a nearby clearing where he jumped from the hovering helicopter, and ran approximately 75 meters under withering small arms fire to the crippled team. Prior to reaching the team's position he was wounded in his right leg, face, and head. Despite these painful injuries, he took charge, repositioning the team members and directing their fire to facilitate the landing of an extraction aircraft, and the loading of wounded and dead team members. He then threw smoke canisters to direct the aircraft to the team's position.

Despite his severe wounds and under intense enemy fire, he carried and dragged half of the wounded team members to the awaiting aircraft. He then provided protective fire by running alongside the aircraft as it moved to pick up the remaining team members. As the enemy's fire intensified, he hurried to recover the body and classified documents on the dead team leader. When he reached the leader's body, Sergeant Benavidez was severely wounded by small arms fire in the abdomen and grenade fragments in his back. At nearly the same moment, the aircraft pilot was mortally wounded, and his helicopter crashed. Although in extremely critical condition due to his multiple wounds, Sergeant Benavidez secured the classified documents and made his way back to the wreckage, where he aided the wounded out of the overturned aircraft, and gathered the stunned survivors into a defensive perimeter.

Under increasing enemy automatic weapons and grenade fire, he moved around the perimeter distributing water and ammunition to his weary men, re-instilling in them a will to live and fight. Facing a build-up of enemy opposition with a beleaguered team, Sergeant Benavidez mustered his strength, began calling in tactical air strikes and directed the fire from supporting gunships to suppress the enemy's fire and so permit another extraction attempt. He was wounded again in his thigh by small arms fire while administering first aid to a wounded team member just before another extraction helicopter was able to land.

His indomitable spirit kept him going as he began to ferry his comrades to the craft. On his second trip with the wounded, he was clubbed from additional wounds to his head and arms before killing his adversary. He then continued under devastating fire to carry the wounded to the helicopter. Upon reaching the aircraft, he spotted and killed two enemy soldiers who were rushing the craft from an angle that prevented the aircraft door gunner from firing upon them. With little strength remaining, he made one last trip to the perimeter to ensure that all classified material had been collected or destroyed, and to bring in the remaining wounded. Only then, in extremely serious condition from numerous wounds and loss of blood, did he allow himself to be pulled into the extraction aircraft.

Sergeant Benavidez' gallant choice to join voluntarily his comrades who were in critical straits, to expose himself constantly to withering enemy fire, and his refusal to be stopped despite numerous severe wounds, saved the lives of at least eight men.[3]

For that amazing act of reckless valor, Roy P. Benavidez received the Congressional Medal of Honor.[4] His story is a great illustration of above and beyond; not the ordinary or the expected.

In professional soccer, when a player scores a goal the crowd will stand, cheer, shout and celebrate the goal; they honour the player who scored it. Similarly, when a goalkeeper repels or blocks a shot, he is honoured for it. Do either of them deserve the honour? No, not really, because both of these players are paid a stack of money to do those things and this is what their club requires of them. It is the duty of the highly-paid players to score goals and fulfill their assigned role. They haven't really done anything that merits honour. Remember, true honour goes to those who go above and beyond the call of duty.

How do we as Christians apply this idea of honour—above and beyond—to our own lives? You may say, "I read my Bible." Good. So you should. "I gave my offering." Excellent! You should do that too. "I pray," or "I was generous to someone and received nothing in return." That is how we are expected to live as Christians; it is our "reasonable service."⁵

Honour comes when we go beyond. Put simply, it is to go the second mile.

When someone is said to have gone the second mile, it is an act of honouring both for the cause for which that mile was "walked" and for the one who walked it. Great churches are not built on the ordinary, but on the second mile principle. Effective and overcoming Christians are those who don't live an ordinary life but will go the second mile. In other words, they don't do simply what they must or are expected to do to be in church, but they go above and beyond and live an extraordinary life.

GOING THE EXTRA MILE

God has called us to live a life that's extraordinary, not ordinary. The difference between an *ordinary* and an *extraordinary* life is the addition of "extra." Someone who goes the second mile gives *extra*—extra time, extra energy or extra in their offering, among other things. Whatever the *extra* is that we add to the *ordinary* in our life is what makes our lives extraordinary. Take marriage, for instance. If our marriages are ordinary and the *extra* is added to them, they will become extraordinary. The same is true of our walk with Christ. If it is ordinary and we think we are ordinary, then we should do the *extra* that will make our lives take on the extraordinary—and that usually means sacrifice.

I remember once reading a particular story reflecting sacrifice that left a lasting impression on me. It took place in the 1950s when a group of five missionaries felt led to journey to the border of Peru and Ecuador to take the good news of the Gospel to a very primitive and dangerous tribe of headhunters; they were committed to winning them for Christ.

It took the five men a great deal of preparation and time to get ready for the journey and to work out exactly how they would reach these remote people. Finally, after many months they set off, managing to set up some base camps. Eventually they entered the jungle, making contact with the tribe. Encouraged and inspired, they returned to make further contact whereupon all five missionaries were killed by some of the tribesmen.

When news of this tragedy was received, many looked upon their trip as a complete failure; but it sparked a willingness in a lot of people to sacrifice everything and go the second mile to serve God. Elizabeth, the wife of James Elliot, one of the five missionaries, returned to the tribe who killed her husband and won them all for Christ—an act beyond the call of duty. When a magazine discovered the five missionaries' story and published it, many young men and women who read the article were greatly moved with a heart-response of "Lord, here am I, send me." I was one of them.

So, what appeared on the surface to be a great waste and failure became, in fact, costly seed sown, which went on to produce a miraculous harvest that continues today. All this was because five men went beyond the call of duty, making the ultimate sacrifice to do something extraordinary with their lives.

In Acts 6 we read of a deacon in the early Church by the name of Stephen, whose extraordinary life paralleled that of those five men. The Church was rapidly growing and a great need emerged as a result. Though already meeting the needs of the people, a complaint arose:

> As the believers rapidly multiplied, there were rumblings of discontent. The Greek-speaking believers complained about the Hebrew-speaking believers, saying that their widows were being discriminated against in the daily distribution of food.[6]

The Church had a population of multiplied thousands and the apostles were trying to deal with this problem of distributing food as well as fulfilling their calling to seek God and preach the Word. Look at what they decided to do:

> So the Twelve called a meeting of all the believers. They said, "We apostles should spend our time teaching the word of God, not running a food program. And so, brothers, select seven men who are well respected and are full of the Spirit and wisdom. We will give them this responsibility. Then we apostles can spend our time in prayer and teaching the word."

Everyone liked this idea, and they chose the following: Stephen (a man full of faith and the Holy Spirit), Philip,

Procorus, Nicanor, Timon, Parmenas, and Nicolas of Antioch (an earlier convert to the Jewish faith). These seven were presented to the apostles, who prayed for them as they laid their hands on them.[7]

Stephen probably was chosen because of what he did. He served voluntarily, likely arriving early to prepare, leaving late to clean up—one of those faithful people who are always there. It is a strong possibility that the biggest rewards in heaven will be for those who faithfully serve the church in some way: setting up, praying for the congregation, caring for the children, and so on. For such qualities of servanthood Stephen was chosen along with the other six. He was full of the Holy Spirit and his role was to distribute food and wait on tables—and, as we'll see in a moment, God greatly rewarded him.

When they reach heaven, there will be many in the church who will receive honour that they never received on the earth for the untold, unseen things, the extra miles perhaps seen only by God. Going the second mile is a sacrifice—but it's where honour is given.

PUBLIC AND PRIVATE HONOUR

Honour is a principle. It is a second mile principle and a moral rule, a standard by which we are to live. In other words, it requires something of us. The whole nature of God is wrapped with honour. God has done everything for us, including the sacrifice of His only Son. All this because of His grace:

Not because of works [not the fulfillment of the Law's demands], lest any man should boast. [It is not the result of what anyone can possibly do, so no one can pride himself in it or take glory to himself.][8]

God's grace is stunning. Where *grace* means unmerited favor, honour is earned.[9] So while there is nothing we could do to deserve God's favor—it is a gift—yet He rewards our work.

There are times where we "feel" we don't deserve God, or we don't deserve His favor. We think something like this: "I didn't read my Bible, so I don't deserve to hear His voice"; or "I didn't give an offering, so I don't deserve to receive a blessing"; or "I didn't pray, so I don't deserve His answered prayer." Does that mean if we do read the Bible, or give in the offering, or pray long hours, we now deserve His favor? If His favor could be earned, then, how much should we pray, give, and sacrifice to earn it? Can we earn heaven as well? Absolutely not; all of our best acts of righteousness are as filthy rags, the Bible says.[10] It is His amazing gift, amazing grace.

This is why we hear angels cry, "Blessing and honour and glory and power belong to the one sitting on the throne and to the Lamb forever and ever."[11]

Still, everything about God gives. He asks for our worship, and as we worship Him, we are blessed. We think we give Him everything—our money, our acts of kindness, our worship. We think that God asks this because He is God, but He uses these things to bless us. He turns it around. Everything He asks of us, it is really to bless us.

Paul mentions how God does "exceedingly abundantly above all that we ask or think."[12] So while we honour Him, He in turn honours us as we serve Him.

It is written in God's Word that Jesus himself will one day reward us for our works on earth. This is difficult to comprehend and yet in Matthew 6:17 we are told that what we do privately to help others, God will reward openly and in public. Still again we are told in Revelation 2:10 that we are to receive a crown depending on the works we do and that this crown is in recognition of these works. Think of it—the same hands that were nailed to the cross will place a crown on our head, and it will be in honour of our service and devotion to Him.[13] How will we respond to such an undeserved act?

The soldiers mentioned at the beginning of this chapter who were awarded their Medal of Honor said they didn't deserve it. They felt guilty because their friends had died and paid with their lives. They didn't understand why they were being honoured. When we receive our crown in heaven, no doubt our response will be similar. Like those in Revelation 4:10–11, we will have an awareness of our unworthiness before the Lord; we will respond with worship and declaration:

The twenty-four elders fall down before Him who sits on the throne and worship Him who lives forever and ever, and cast their crowns before the throne, saying, "You [alone] are worthy, O Lord [our God], to receive glory and honour and power; for You created all things, and by Your will they exist and were created."[14]

Yet this truth remains so—there is nothing we do for God and for others in private that He won't reward us for openly and publicly. So how did God reward Stephen?

Acts 6:10 says that Stephen spoke with wisdom and the Spirit and that none of those present in the synagogue could argue or stand against what he spoke. The time came when so many people were listening to Stephen that the Sanhedrin (the Jewish religious leaders or council of that day) were determined to silence him. They plotted against him by bribing others to lie about him and bring him before the Sanhedrin to be judged. When asked if the accusations were true, Stephen didn't respond directly; instead, he used the opportunity to challenge them, saying:

> "You stubborn people! You are heathen at heart and deaf to the truth. Must you forever resist the Holy Spirit? That's what your ancestors did, and so do you! Name one prophet your ancestors didn't persecute! They even killed the ones who predicted the coming of the Righteous One—the Messiah whom you betrayed and murdered. You deliberately disobeyed God's law, even though you received it from the hands of angels." The Jewish leaders were infuriated by Stephen's accusation, and they shook their fists at him in rage.[15]

This attitude and spirit still pervades our world today. There are always those who do not want change and resist it vehemently when others seek to bring it, as Stephen brought to those religious leaders. There are people all around us who say, "Things will never change. That's just the way it is." They have forfeited hope in exchange for cynicism and negativity. Stephen said, "That's what your ancestors did and so do you."

Many times children end up like their parents, making the same mistakes and decisions. But it doesn't have to be that way any longer. There is something new! The answer has come. Christ came so that we do not have to follow after the patterns of our fathers and forefathers as they did in the Old Testament. Now there is a new generation—the Christ generation created anew.

Stephen's accusations infuriated the Jewish leaders and they shook their fists and ground their teeth with rage. What Stephen said next angered them even more."But Stephen, full of the Holy Spirit, looked up to heaven and saw the glory of God, and Jesus *standing* at the right hand of God. 'Look,' he said, 'I see heaven open and the Son of Man *standing* at the right hand of God.'"[16] At this, Stephen was dragged from the city and stoned to death by them.

The significance of Stephen seeing Jesus standing is related to the protocol of a king and his throne. In the book of Esther, when Esther chose to enter unannounced in the presence of her husband, the king, to speak to him, she was confronted with the risk of death because there was no prior invitation. When she did approach the king, he extended his sceptre toward her, a symbol of his authority.[17] This was an act of mercy and grace, accepting Esther's presence. Had the king failed to do so, the result for her would have been very grave indeed.

When a king stood in the presence of another, it was an act of high honour toward that person. So, just before Stephen was stoned to death, he saw Jesus Christ *standing* at God's right hand. The King stood in Stephen's presence—the King of kings and Lord of lords was honouring Stephen.

God honours those who honour Him.

Chapter 6

STOLEN HONOUR

It is better to deserve honours and not have them than to have them and not deserve them.

—Mark Twain

In Washington, DC, another memorial I like to visit is the Vietnam Veterans Memorial. There are many names are written on the monument wall, including those of some friends of mine. This memorial has great personal significance to me but not for that reason alone.

This particular monument is not immediately visible to the visitor—one could walk or drive straight past it without any clue of its location. That's because it is below ground level in a very large park called the National Mall. As you approach the monument, however, it suddenly appears as an enormous wall of granite engraved with all the names of those who lost their lives in the Vietnam War. On the web site of the U.S. Department of Interior's National Park Service, this explanation of the design is found:

"Deliberately setting aside the controversies of the war, the Vietnam Veterans Memorial honours the men and women who served when their Nation called upon them. The designer, Maya Lin, felt that 'the politics had eclipsed the veterans, their service and their lives.' She kept the design elegantly simple to 'allow everyone to respond and remember.'"[1]

Once you see this magnificent memorial, it's hard not to remember. More than 50,000 names confront you; every one carved into highly-polished granite. Each name represents a life, a soul, a sacrifice. As you draw closer to read the names, the black granite surface takes on the qualities of a mirror and you begin to see your reflection in it. As I stood there at that moment I was forced to ask myself, *Do I deserve the freedom I've been given?* These men and women gave their lives for it.

Moving along to the granite wall of the monument, I saw the names and my reflection again in it. Then something extraordinary happened. Through the names and my reflection emerged the image of one of the soldiers who lost his life in this war, and then another one and another…looking back at me from that wall.

Immediately my thoughts went to those 50,000 who gave their lives for our country—for all of us. For me. It was a profound moment.

Not too far from there I came across another arresting memorial, this one to the Korean War veterans. Written on it in large letters is this confronting statement: "Freedom Is Not Free." The National Park Service also expounds on this memorial, saying:

"Here, one finds the expression of American gratitude to those who restored freedom to South Korea. Nineteen stainless steel sculptures stand silently under the watchful eye of a sea of faces upon a granite wall—reminders of the human cost of defending freedom. These elements all bear witness to the patriotism, devotion to duty, and courage of Korean War veterans."[2]

Pondering the engraved statement, I thought, *How true...freedom is not free. Someone, somewhere at sometime paid a great price for all the freedoms we enjoy today.*

I eventually pulled myself from my thoughts and turned to leave. That's when I noticed a small gathering of men who were quite obviously war veterans as they were wearing medals on their chests. These men were selling souvenirs and mementos of the monument. My impulse was to go up to them and express my thanks for their enormous sacrifice and maybe to purchase something as an act of honour and respect; after all, these were some of the ones who had fought out there—to them this is not simply a monument of their war, but a constant reminder of their pain, sacrifice, pride, comradeship and of the freedom in which we now live.

Sometime after this visit, I was with a veteran of the Vietnam War, a man, who in many ways was an inspiration for me to write this book, Lieutenant Colonel Randy Elms. He is a faithful follower of Christ and a dear friend. I had been discussing my experience at the National Mall and in particular my encounter with the veterans who were selling mementos at the wall. He said to me, "Let me tell you about a few of those men who sell souvenirs at the monument. Some of them, not all, are fake!" I couldn't believe what I was hearing. The idea that someone would betray people's trust and trade on gratitude and sentiment by falsely claiming to have fought in that war, assuming an honour that belonged to another, was inconceivable to me.

It woke me up to something—stolen honour. Those men were taking and claiming what they did not deserve or earn.

Shortly after this I found an article in a US newspaper that spoke about the search for false war heroes. The article highlighted one particular man who was pictured dressed in full uniform with many medals decorating his chest. This man had been going about from place to place and people would honour him for his service. He received countless invitations to functions and events and many gifts and words of gratitude. Sadly, when he was asked why he did all this he simply replied, "So people would buy me a drink." But it was all a charade.

A hero's recognition and reward does not belong to an imposter. Such an act brings dishonour to those they are pretending to be. Honour is not something to be traded upon or stolen. It belongs to those who are deserving of it.

Stolen honour is distressing to the deserving, but it can be devastating to the undeserving: "Such people dig a deep hole, then fall in it themselves."[3]

AVOIDING THE DITCH

Admiral Jeremy Michael Boorda had an outstanding and unique career in the United States Navy with over 30 years of service in North America. A recruit at the age of 17, he began his career as a typist in a Navy personnel office in San Diego and was promoted through the ranks until, at 23, he became an officer. Eventually at the age of 52, Jeremy "Mike" Boorda was promoted to admiral. He was the first person to ever achieve progressing through the ranks to this level. In fact, his career was so outstanding that not only was he the first soldier to become an admiral, but he was nominated for candidacy as head of Joint Chiefs of Staff. In other words, if he was successful, he would reach the highest military office in the United States. Mike Boorda warmly accepted the nomination.

Nominees for this office are subject to intense scrutiny and revision of their lives and career and it was no different for Admiral Boorda. It is customary to scrutinize with the utmost detail, using a magnifying glass to inspect photographs for such things as a loose thread, the presentation of medals and so on, as absolutely everything had to be impeccable when in formal appearance.

As a background check was begun and a particular official photograph was under review, something irregular drew the attention of the reviewer: a bronze medal from a battle in Vietnam where Boorda served as Admiral on board various battleships that were active during the war.

It was correct that he should be wearing this medal; however, another small brass "V" hung below it. This "V" signifies valor and is earned by serving in hand-to-hand combat in battle. Admiral Boorda did not engage in this kind of combat and so was not entitled to wear this medal.

A rigorous investigation was immediately initiated and Admiral Boorda was subjected to intense questioning concerning the reason he wore this particular decoration when it appeared that he did not deserve to. The ensuing controversy soon became a scandal for what was already a harrowing time for the United States Navy. Admiral Boorda's candidacy was immediately revoked and talk of demotion was in the air.

At one point, a 2:30 p.m. meeting was scheduled between the Washington bureau chief of *Newsweek* magazine and Admiral Boorda. However, at 2:05 p.m. the admiral's body was found "in a side yard next to his quarters at the Washington Navy Yard. He was pronounced dead at DC General Hospital a few minutes later."[4] He had reportedly taken his own life because of overwhelming shame over the dishonour his actions had brought on his beloved Navy.

Thirty years of an outstanding and exemplary career ended in disgrace because this man claimed recognition for something he hadn't earned.

Proverbs 24:3 says, in the *Amplified Bible*,

"Through skilful and godly Wisdom is a house (a life, a home, a family) built, and by understanding it is established [on a sound and good foundation]."

Wisdom builds, foolishness is destructive.

Something else the Bible says about this issue was written by King Solomon, someone many consider to be the wisest man who ever lived.

"Wise words bring approval, but fools are destroyed by their own words."[5]

With one foolish decision, Admiral Boorda threw away the extraordinary career he had worked so hard to achieve. How many people spend years and years working, raising children, building family, friends and a life, only to destroy it all with a single, foolish decision? Others will devote years of sacrifice to study and pursue a career path, yet a foolish decision will cost them everything they worked so hard for.

By wearing that small brass "V" medal, Admiral Boorda had taken the credit for something that someone else had sacrificed for.

Have you had another person take the credit for something you worked hard at? Have you ever been given the credit for something you didn't do? Stealing honour will end up leading you into a ditch.

The book of Esther tells of when a man called Haman looked for undeserved credit that belonged to a Hebrew man named Mordecai—and ended up in the ditch he had dug for Mordecai.

At first, Mordecai was one of the doorkeepers of the king's court and Haman hated him because Mordecai refused to bow and pay homage to him. An unexpected decision the king made regarding Mordecai sent Haman's hate over the edge.

> "[One night,] unable to sleep, the king was flipping through some records in the royal archives when he read of the assassination plot that Mordecai had thwarted. Surprised to learn that Mordecai had never been rewarded for this deed, the king asked Haman what should be done to properly thank a hero. *Haman thought the king must be talking about him, and so he described a lavish reward.* The king agreed, but to Haman's shock and utter humiliation, he learned that Mordecai was the person to be so honoured."[6]

Haman was so outraged that he devised a plot to kill Mordecai by tricking the king into decreeing that on a certain date all Jews in the land would be killed. Eventually Esther revealed Haman's treachery to the king, who had him executed on the very gallows that Haman had constructed himself for Mordecai's demise.

In 2 Kings 5, we see another example of a man who took something he didn't deserve and ended up in a ditch—Gehazi, the servant of Elisha. Gehazi was present when Elisha healed Naaman, a mighty warrior and commander of the king's army, who had contracted leprosy. Naaman had learned of Elisha from his wife's maid. Upon hearing of Naaman's illness, the young Jewish girl had told him of a prophet in Israel who could heal him of the deadly disease. So Naaman went with his horses and chariots to Elisha's house.

When the prophet told Naaman to go wash in the Jordan River seven times, Naaman got angry, started complaining and left in a rage because he expected Elisha to do something spectacular to heal him. When his officers reasoned with him to do as Elisha had asked, he finally complied "and his skin became as healthy as [the skin of] a young child's, and he was healed!"[7]

Naaman was so grateful, that he wanted to reward Elisha and said to the prophet, "Now I know that there is no God in all the world except in Israel. So please accept a gift from your servant."

But Elisha replied, "As surely as the LORD lives, whom I serve, I will not accept any gifts." And though Naaman urged him to take the gift, Elisha refused.

Gehazi, who was standing nearby, had other ideas and upon Elisha's refusal made a foolish decision:

Gehazi, the servant of Elisha, the man of God, said to himself, "My master should not have let this Aramean get away without accepting any of his gifts. As surely as the LORD lives, I will chase after him and get something from him." So Gehazi set off after Naaman.

When Naaman saw Gehazi running after him, he climbed down from his chariot and went to meet him. "Is everything all right?" Naaman asked.

"Yes," Gehazi said, "but my master has sent me to tell you that two young prophets from the hill country of Ephraim have just arrived. He would like 75 pounds of silver and two sets of clothing to give to them."

"By all means, take twice as much silver," Naaman insisted. He gave him two sets of clothing, tied up the money in two bags, and sent two of his servants to carry the gifts for Gehazi. But when they arrived at the citadel, Gehazi took the gifts from the servants and sent the men back. Then he went and hid the gifts inside the house.

When Gehazi returned to Elisha, Elisha asked Gehazi where he'd been and Gehazi made another foolish decision—he lied to Elisha, saying he hadn't been anywhere.

But Elisha asked him, "Don't you realize that I was there in spirit when Naaman stepped down from his chariot to meet you? Is this the time to receive money and clothing, olive groves and vineyards, sheep and cattle, and male and female servants? Because you have done this, you and your descendants will suffer from Naaman's leprosy forever." When Gehazi left the room, he was covered with leprosy; his skin was white as snow.[8]

What could be the motive for someone to want the honour that others have or deserve? Honour comes at a price, personal sacrifice, doing right in the face of opposition. Some, like Gehazi, look to receive undeserved reward and acknowledgment. Others become green-eyed when someone receives more credit than they do—that's called jealousy, a costly thing to hook up with. For one man in the Bible it cost him his throne and his life.

BE FAITHFUL AND RECEIVE

When the victorious Israelite army was returning home after David had killed the Philistine, women from all the towns of Israel came out to meet King Saul. They sang and danced for joy with tambourines and cymbals. This was their song:

"Saul has killed his thousands and David his ten thousands!"

This made Saul very angry. "What's this?" he said. "They credit David with ten thousands and me with only thousands. Next they'll be making him their king!" So from that time on Saul kept a jealous eye on David.

The very next day a tormenting spirit from God overwhelmed Saul, and he began to rave in his house like a madman. David was playing the harp, as he did each day. But Saul had a spear in his hand and he suddenly hurled it at David, intending to pin him to the wall. But David escaped him twice.[9]

Saul became enraged with jealousy—and jealousy can kill. Jealousy is a feeling of unhappiness and anger because another person has something or someone that you want. It has been called the green-eyed monster, and with good reason. People can literally be consumed, eaten up by jealousy. They want what others have and are willing to take, at all costs, what others have earned. Yet when it comes to honour, we are to honour where honour is due.[10] *Due* means where it is owed, expected, deserved.

Some may actually feel they deserve what they did not earn, the applause for work someone else did or the medal others received, as in Admiral Boorda's case. Or as in Gehazi's sad story, they tell a lie to receive finances not due them. The apostle Paul said, "Love is not jealous."[11] Love gives, even at the cost of self. Lust takes, at the cost of others. When we see what others have and lust after it, that is a jealous spirit. It can become all-consuming. King Saul is a classic example.

Here's the point: at the core of stolen honour is a jealous spirit, which is so opposite of what we are taught in the Bible that we are to be. Luke 16:12, for instance, talks about being faithful with that which is another man's.

Jesus spoke a parable in Matthew 20:1–16. It was about workers in a vineyard. The owner of the vineyard set off early to find some men to employ in his vineyard for the day. He found some men and agreed to pay them the normal daily wage before sending them out to work. Then at nine o'clock, while he was at the markets, he saw some unemployed men whom he also offered work in his vineyard. He agreed with them that he would "pay them whatever was right" at the end of the day.[12] He did the same thing again at midday and again at three o'clock in the afternoon. Again at five o'clock, with only an hour left for the workday, he found still more men who had no work and so he employed them for the final hour.

When the time came for the workers to receive their pay, all of the men were paid exactly the same amount. Some of them became angry:

When they received their pay, they protested to the owner, "Those people worked only one hour, and yet you've paid them just as much as you paid us who worked all day in the scorching heat."[13]

Does this seem fair or just to you? It has everything to do with the compassion and grace of God.

I once heard a story about a famous actress who was preparing to attend an Oscars award night many years ago and she went to a beauty salon where it is said that she paid $5,000 for a manicure, $5,000 for a pedicure and another $5,000 for her makeup. By the time she left the salon, she'd paid thousands of dollars. When the press discovered this, she was criticized and they asked her, "How can you spend so much money on yourself at a salon?" Her answer was stunning: "The woman who fixed my hair is a single mother who is in debt. The one who did my nails has two kids and a lot of needs and the others are the same." In other words, she was implying, "If I want to help these women, what is that to you?"

The response of the vineyard owner in Jesus' parable was similar:

"Friend, I haven't been unfair! Didn't you agree to work all day for the usual wage? Take your money and go. I wanted to pay this last worker the same as you. Is it against the law for me to do what I want with my money? Should you be jealous because I am kind to others?"[14]

Why do people get upset when others are blessed saying, "Why them and not me?" We should rejoice when others are blessed and honoured. Not only is it biblical, but it is to our benefit. Ed Cole, international speaker and author, describes the benefits, saying, "Being faithful in that which is another man's qualifies us to receive our own."

When we can stop trying to take that which belongs to another— take credit, take recognition, take the applause, take honour— because of a jealous spirit; when we can stop being upset when someone else is blessed and instead, rejoice over another person's promotion, blessing, or possessions, God can trust us with our own.

REACH YOUR CALLING AND DESTINY

In Acts 4, the early Church was in its first days. The message of the Gospel was being preached, but it wasn't enough to simply get people saved; a very real crisis of poverty existed and the Christians wanted to help. A ticket to heaven is wonderful and necessary, but people have to live on the earth in the meantime and poverty is a curse from which Jesus died to deliver us. The response in Acts 4 was the flowering of generosity throughout the community in Jerusalem.

A follower of Jesus named Barnabas sold land he had received as an inheritance and brought the proceeds to the apostles.[15] Barnabas came with help and was acknowledged for his generosity. There was need and the people of the church were able to meet it.

Now let's look at what happened shortly after that in Acts 5:

But there was a certain man named Ananias who, with his wife, Sapphira, sold some property. He brought part of the money to the apostles, claiming it was the full amount. With his wife's consent, he kept the rest.

Then Peter said, "Ananias, why have you let Satan fill your heart? You lied to the Holy Spirit, and you kept some of the money for yourself. The property was yours to sell or not sell, as you wished. And after selling it, the money was also yours to give away. How could you do a thing like this? You weren't lying to us but to God!"

As soon as Ananias heard these words, he fell to the floor and died. Everyone who heard about it was terrified. Then some young men got up, wrapped him in a sheet, and took him out and buried him.

About three hours later his wife came in, not knowing what had happened. Peter asked her, "Was this the price you and your husband received for your land?"

"Yes," she replied, "that was the price."

And Peter said, "How could the two of you even think of conspiring to test the Spirit of the Lord like this? The young men who buried your husband are just outside the door, and they will carry you out, too."

Instantly, she fell to the floor and died. When the young men came in and saw that she was dead, they carried her out and buried her beside her husband.[16]

Ananias and Sapphira watched the example of Barnabas but rather than do likewise, they falsified their offering, pretending to be as generous as he had been, but they lied.

The issue is not that we are expected to give everything. Ananias and Sapphira could just as easily have been honest and said that their offering was a portion of the sale of an inheritance to be used for the poor; but instead they lied. Their motive was the desire for honour and recognition for something they had not done; pretending to be something they weren't.

Here is why this matter was judged so severely: This was the genesis of the Church, the beginning, and already pretenders were showing up   and had pretenders and hypocrites been allowed to infiltrate, the Church would have been contaminated.

Jesus Christ loves His Church and gave His life for it. Our response should be to honour it by guarding against anything that has the potential to corrupt or damage it. Doing so will help us in fulfilling our destiny.

The name Barnabas means "Son of encouragement."[17] His life is rewarded in the Scriptures as having fulfilled his calling and destiny. The name Ananias means "the grace of God"[18] and Sapphira's name means "woman of beauty."[19] Their names showed they had a destiny, yet they never reached it because they tried to steal another's honour.

How many people have a purpose, a call, but never reach their potential because they try to take recognition or honour that is not theirs? They dishonoured their names, their church and Jesus himself by coveting someone else's honour. It caused them to lie and deceive and it cost them their lives—they forfeited their calling and destiny.

In the Bible, people's names were significant and reflected their bearer's calling in life. Take the example of the twelve spies who were sent by Moses to survey and report on Canaan, the Promised Land.[20] Most Christians are familiar with the story— two of the spies came back with a good report on being able to take the land and the other ten said it was impossible.

When asked the name of the two spies with the good report, a lot of people immediately say Joshua and Caleb, which is correct. When asked the names of the other ten, however, there's often silence. Why? The two with the good report are honoured still to this day. We remember their names because of their actions. They had a different report than the ten. They believed God. God honoured that belief—they were the only two to see the promise. They stood against the popular opinion, against the crowd. Interestingly, Joshua means "Jehovah is salvation,"[21] and he fulfilled his destiny. Caleb means "Dog."[22] Looking at Caleb's life, we can see the connection: at age 80 he faced the mountain he had waited to obtain for 40 years and declared "even though I am 80 years old and there are giants there, give me my mountain."[23] Caleb was like a fighting dog who laid hold of his inheritance despite the size of his opponents.

Could the ten have been honoured? Their names suggest they too had potential.

- Shammua—Renowned, or heard of God.

- Shaphat— Judge, to judge or avenge.

- Igal— Avenger

- Palti— Delieverance from the Lord

- Gaddiel—The fortune of God

- Gaddi—Fortunate

- Ammiel—People of God

- Sethur—Hidden

- Nahbi— Also means hidden

- Geuel—Majesty of God[24]

Obviously, they could have been honoured and remembered as well. God presented them with an opportunity to go the extra mile by stepping up and believing against what they saw. These men had destinies that they didn't reach. How sad when people throw away their potential and destiny because of fear, pride or pretence. Such things can ruin a person's life.

Ananias and Sapphira tried to steal honour. These ten men just disappeared from any relevance. Gone. We hear no more about them. Few things will frustrate a man more than regret, when it's all over, to say what could have been, what should have been, what if, if only.

What if Haman had sought honour in an honourable way? What if Saul had loved David and his abilities instead of having a jealous spirit? For Admiral Boorda, what could have been a distinguished career, if only.... Gahazi, should have been Elisha's successor, he served Elisha as Elisha served Elijah—if only.... Ananias and Sapphira, if only.... What about the men selling souvenirs and mementos at the war memorial, what if instead of stealing the honour of others and wearing the uniform and medals they didn't deserve, what if they used that energy to serve?

This is enough for me. It is not about seeking another person's credit or honour; it's about serving God and others and receiving our own. That often involves sacrifice.

Chapter 7

THE OTHER SIDE OF SACRIFICE

A nation who fails to honour its heroes will soon have no heroes to honour.

—*Winston Churchill*

So many Americans didn't understand the Vietnam War and some even protested against it. Countless young men and women lost their lives, never to return home. Others who returned carried great burdens and trauma from what they had witnessed and experienced. Neither the horrors nor the casualties of that war were respected or acknowledged.

These returning soldiers were abused, spat upon and shamed, and their sacrifice was unappreciated and uncelebrated. The confronting truth of such injustice is the enormous debt it protracted—over 50,000 soldiers died in battle during this war, but not many realize that more than 9,000 who fought and survived ended up committing suicide after they returned.[1] These service men and women were obligated to fight for their country, came to serve as their duty to country and for freedom, but were repaid for their sacrifice without the "thank you" they deserved—a homecoming without honour.

It was a long time coming, but in 1982 that wrong was righted through a life-changing event that took place for many soldiers who had served in the Vietnam War—the Vietnam Veterans Memorial was dedicated in Washington, DC, to honour U.S. service members who had fought, died, or were unaccounted for (M.I.A.) while serving in Vietnam/Southeast Asia during that horrendous conflict. A decorated Vietnam War veteran came up with the plan to build the memorial and made personal sacrifices to raise millions of dollars for it, beginning with over a couple thousand of his own dollars donated.[2]

We live in an unjust world. We see people being treated unfairly, we see the unjust actions of others and it bothers us. We recognize the injustice and we desire that it be made right. When the strong take advantage of the weak, when the defenceless are abused, when those who've made great sacrifices are dishonoured instead of honoured, it troubles us deeply. Imagine how all of it must affect the heart of God. Injustice is thriving in the world, but when someone makes a sacrifice to correct an injustice and brings justice—as did the Vietnam veteran who built the memorial—it can be life-changing for all involved.

We have an orphanage in Lima, Peru. The children who shelter there have been subjected to traumas and abuse that no human being should ever have to experience, let alone a child. But the fact is that no matter how tragic or unjust, we cannot change these children's past. We can, however, alter the course of their future by making wrong, right.

Similarly, we have another home there for girls as young as 13 who have been raped, beaten and traded like goods. It breaks our hearts to see these precious lives so damaged and although we cannot wipe out what has happened, we can intervene by bringing hope and solution, changing the course of their lives.

Without faith, we cannot possibly please God,[3] but James 2:26 says, "Faith is dead without good works," merciful, loving, sacrificial works that glorify God and benefit others. Deeds like these are recorded by Him—the unseen, unacknowledged good deeds will be rewarded by God. Jesus talked about a reward and gave the meaning of sacrifice in this passage:

> Peter…[said]: "We left everything we owned and followed you, didn't we?" "Yes," said Jesus, "and you won't regret it. No one who has sacrificed home, spouse, brothers and sisters, parents, children—whatever—will lose out. It will all come back multiplied many times over in your lifetime. And then the bonus of eternal life!"[4]

Remember, without faith, we cannot possibly please God. To sacrifice is to give up something of value to you, to help another person—and honour is always on the other side of sacrifice.

SACRIFICE, FRUIT, AND HONOUR

When my family moved to Peru in 1983 to serve as missionaries, I often looked to a few older, seasoned missionaries for counsel. One such man was Earl Kellum. Earl had served as a missionary in Mexico for 50 years and had raised thousands of leaders and hundreds of churches. He had begun opening churches in Central and South America and when I had the opportunity to meet him he was an elderly and humble man who had barely enough to pay for his meals. Earl was a modern-day hero; a missionary who sacrificed much and produced much fruit.

One day when we were talking, I asked Earl about what his service to the mission had cost him. He told me how, although he had lost his wife and his children on the mission field, he had no regrets. "If I had to do it all over again I'd still say yes to serving Him," were his words.

Later on, watching the "I Heart Revolution" movie,[5] I remembered another missionary called Brother Andrew. Andrew had seen great sacrifice and great fruit for God's Kingdom—he had been the catalyst for so many open doors of opportunity for the Gospel. In an interview he was asked about all the time and sacrifice he had made and he interrupted saying, "'Sacrifice? Sacrifice? What sacrifice? Where would I be if it weren't for Jesus' sacrifice?"

Hebrews 12:1–2 sums up the idea and attitude of sacrifice in light of the fact that there are very real things in life that we must endure when we follow Christ and seek to live according to His calling. Verse 1 says:

> Since we are surrounded by such a huge crowd of witnesses to the life of faith, let us strip off every weight that slows us down, especially the sin that so easily trips us up. And let us run with endurance the race God has set before us. We are yet another generation in a successive line of believers with a God-ordained "race to run" and hindrances to throw off and overcome. How do we do this when things get really tough or we just don't know what is ahead of us or when we wonder if the sacrifice and endurance are really worth the cost?

> We do this by keeping our eyes on Jesus, the champion who initiates and perfects our faith. Because of the joy awaiting him, he endured the cross, disregarding its shame. Now he is seated in the place of honour beside God's throne.[6]

Jesus disregarded the sacrifice He had to make and the shame He had to endure because He understood what was on the other side of it—salvation by grace for all mankind. His eyes were on us.

> You know the generous grace of our Lord Jesus Christ. Though he was rich, yet for your sakes he became poor, so that by his poverty he could make you rich.[7]

Jesus became God incarnate; a man subjected to humanity's weaknesses and hardship, surrendering His divinity and glory for our sakes, able to endure indescribable hardship and pain because He knew the reward that the sacrifice of His obedience would produce.

Do you think that Jesus would have even an ounce of regret for giving up His divinity and dying on the cross for your sins and mine? Salvation for mankind has been secured and now His place of honour has been restored.

Paul said in 2 Timothy 2:10:

"Therefore I [am ready to] persevere and stand my ground with patience and endure everything for the sake of the elect [God's chosen], so that they too may obtain [the] salvation which is in Christ Jesus, with the reward of eternal glory."

These are not the words of a man who is struggling with regret but a man who has made a decision of conviction enabling him to endure everything for our sakes. Paul's eyes and heart were fixed on Jesus and the reward His sacrifice would achieve.

Hebrews 11, thought by some to have been written by Paul, is known as the Heroes of Faith chapter. Those listed in this "who's who" of biblical faith heroes faced everything from the mouths of lions, to torture, to sword and fire, and yet from scripture it's safe to assume that they had no regrets for the sacrifices they made.

All these people died still believing what God had promised them. They did not receive what was promised, but they saw it all from a distance and welcomed it. They agreed that they were foreigners and nomads here on earth. Obviously people who say such things are looking forward to a country they can call their own. If they had longed for the country they came from, they could have gone back. But they were looking for a better place, a heavenly homeland.[9]

When I read this, I remember again the words of my missionary friend Earl: "I have no regrets." Would this be the response of Abel for offering the better sacrifice than his brother, Cain?[10] Do you think Enoch had regrets for his intimate walk with God?[11] How about Noah, who undoubtedly was mocked and ridiculed during the years he built the ark since it had never rained before?[12] Or Abraham, who left his homeland and all that was familiar and comfortable to go to an unknown and unspecified place at God's request.[13] What about Moses, who went from being Prince of Egypt to desert nomad?[14] No regrets. How is that possible?

"Abraham did it by keeping his eye on an unseen city with real, eternal foundations—the City designed and built by God."[15]

[Moses] thought it was better to suffer for the sake of Christ than to own the treasures of Egypt, for he was looking ahead to his great reward.[16]

Abraham, Moses, and the rest were not looking to a reward on the earth but were looking to heaven and an eternal reward.

That mind-set is wonderfully illustrated in this story of a young couple with little children who, many years ago, felt the call to be missionaries in Africa. In those days there were no airplanes or comfortable transport to such remote places and yet they were determined in their call to evangelize Africa. As they prepared to leave they were told not to pack luggage, just a coffin because that's how they'd return (such comforting, encouraging words!).

Nevertheless, they endured much hardship on their sea journey to Africa and began their life as missionaries on the field. Through the hard years, he buried his wife and one of his sons on the mission field. As his other son grew he decided to send him to America to study while he remained in Africa and continued with his missionary work. Consequently, he didn't see his son for many years. Meanwhile his son completed his studies and began his career.

Eventually this missionary was due to retire and return to the shores of America. As his son awaited his arrival on the docks, the ship arrived and the passengers began to disembark, beginning with first class and working down from there. Dignitaries proceeded to walk from the boat accompanied by the welcoming music of a band, confetti and fanfare. Finally after the band had ceased and the celebrations ended, his father stepped foot onto the dock.

Tears filled the son's eyes as he exclaimed, "Dad, it's not right! No one else came and there was no one to celebrate your return and to receive you—there was no music and no one from your church came to greet you!" To this, the father looked into his son's eyes with understanding and compassion and said, "Son, I'm not home yet." The father knew that one day there would be a celebration and that he would receive his reward; he was looking to heaven, not earth.

He understood that his recognition was still ahead of him when he would arrive at the gates of heaven, so fulfilling his calling was not a sacrifice.

David Livingstone, a nineteenth century Scottish missionary, had that same attitude. He once said, "If a commission by an earthly king is considered a honour, how can a commission by a Heavenly king be considered a sacrifice?"[17]

In other words, if we consider an appointment or commission by a president or king to be the greatest honour and compliment, how is it then that we regard the Great Commission[18] and calling of the King of kings[19] any less?

After the death, burial and resurrection of Jesus Christ, and before He ascended to heaven, Jesus commissioned His disciples, telling them:

> "I have been given all authority in heaven and on earth. Therefore, go and make disciples of all the nations, baptizing them in the name of the Father and the Son and the Holy Spirit. Teach these new disciples to obey all the commands I have given you. And be sure of this: I am with you always, even to the end of the age."[20]

All who receive Jesus as Savior and Lord are commissioned by Him to reach the world with the good news of the gospel. We will invariably encounter troubles and dangers along the way,[21] but victory is always on the other side of a battle. Honour is always on the other side of sacrifice.

WHERE'S YOUR FOCUS?

"Be convinced that to be happy means to be free and that to be free means to be brave. Therefore do not take lightly the perils of war."

—Thucydides

In comparison to World War II where a foot soldier saw 50 days of combat per year, in the Vietnam War a soldier saw 240 days of combat in the same time. The Vietnam War was also a more intense and violent war that incurred a much larger number of casualties. Some of these soldiers were teenagers who, as we've seen, returned to no honour, no appreciation for their sacrifice and no respect. Still, they were victorious because they had been willing to fight. There is no victory in life without the willingness to fight for something.

As British philosopher John Stewart Mill put it, "War is an ugly thing, but not the ugliest of things. The decayed and degraded state of moral and patriotic feeling which thinks that nothing is worth war is much worse. The person who has nothing for which he is willing to fight, nothing which is more important than his own personal safety, is a miserable creature and has no chance of being free unless made and kept so by the exertions of better men than himself."[22]

Some things are worth fighting for—our families, our children, and our faith—yet many in the church want victory but not the fight. They want peace but avoid the battle. Battles are inevitable because we live in dangerous times where the enemy is after our values, and everything else worth fighting for. That's nothing new.

Even in Bible times the enemy—the devil[23]— was after the same thing. Here's one well-known incident from Scripture.

> The Philistines now mustered their army for battle and camped between Socoh in Judah and Azekah at Ephes-dammim. Saul countered by gathering his troops near the valley of Elah. So the Philistines and Israelites faced each other on opposite hills, with the valley between them.[24]

During the time this was going on a young Hebrew lad called David was sent off by his father to supply cheese sandwiches to his brothers at the battlefront. He was not permitted to fight, only to tend to his father's sheep and to deliver food. David arrived at the battlefield and was talking with his brothers but quickly assessed the situation when the enemy's champion, Goliath, came out and taunted the army of Israel.

> "Why are you all coming out to fight?" [Goliath] called. "I am the Philistine champion, but you are only the servants of Saul. Choose one man to come down here and fight me! If he kills me, then we will be your slaves. But if I kill him, you will be our slaves! I defy the armies of Israel today! Send me a man who will fight me!"[25]

Goliath's detailed description in 1 Samuel 17 reveals a lot about the unusual reaction of Saul's troops. Goliath was over nine feet tall! He wore a bronze helmet, and his bronze coat of mail weighed 125 pounds. He also wore bronze leg armor, and he carried a bronze javelin on his shoulder. The shaft of his spear was as heavy and thick as a weaver's beam, tipped with an iron spearhead that weighed 15 pounds. His armor bearer walked ahead of him carrying a shield.[26]

The Israelite forces were fully aware of Goliath's profile, this being the cause of their present malaise—overcome with intimidation and fear. Therein lay the problem: *they knew more about their enemy and his capabilities than about God and His promises.* As a result, the enemy loomed larger in their estimation than God. It's still that way for many today.

Now as then, we are experts on the enemy, how strong and how tall he is. For example, when spoken to, some people can readily give an account of all the bad in their lives. Yet God's consistent promise is that He is for us and so in comparison to Him, no one stands a chance against us—not even a giant![27]

For forty days Goliath shouted his defiant challenge every morning and evening. Interestingly those were the times when Israel would pray and sacrifice—meaning the presence of God is where we find His promises and also the area the enemy will target. His goal is to keep us from accessing God's presence. He will try to convince us that our finances are beyond help, that our marriage is hopeless, that this time the problem is just too big. So rather than focus on God and His Word, we start to give our attention and our conviction to these things.

God promises us that "we can say with confidence, 'The LORD is my helper, so I will have no fear. What can mere people do to me?'"[28] Fear, however, will begin to take hold when the promises and presence of God are absent.

The Israelite army was trapped in a valley for forty days and nights, bombarded with the voice of the enemy, Goliath. The next thing you know, young David came up on the scene fresh from worshipping God and shepherding his father's sheep, to be confronted with the same intimidating voice. But his focus wasn't on the formidable giant or the odds. He had his eyes on the Lord and the reward.

> "Have you seen the giant?" the men asked. "He comes out each day to defy Israel. The king has offered a huge reward to anyone who kills him. He will give that man one of his daughters for a wife, and the man's entire family will be exempted from paying taxes!"[29]

God is like-minded. He honours those of His own who sacrifice, who have risen, stood and been victorious over the giants in their lives. These are heroes of faith.

DOORWAY TO DESTINY

Earlier we looked at the Hebrew root word for "honour," which is *kabod*, and how its meaning implies weight or heaviness. This Hebrew word is also translated "glory." In other words, there is a glory to honour. After a battle, celebration and glory go to the victors. When we live an honourable life, glory and celebration will surely follow. There are those who seek the glory and honour without the fight, but any reward in these cases is shallow and short-lived. Honour and glory can be a driving motivator to continue against all odds.

King Saul had offered a great reward for the man who slayed Goliath—the king's daughter, tax-exemption for life, riches...glory. Still, only one person—a young shepherd boy—was motived to fight for it. When he did, God gave him the victory.

> "Today the LORD will conquer you [Goliath], and I [David] will kill you and cut off your head. And then I will give the dead bodies of your men to the birds and wild animals, and the whole world will know that there is a God in Israel! And everyone assembled here will know that the LORD rescues his people, but not with sword and spear. This is the LORD's battle, and he will give you to us!"

> As Goliath moved closer to attack, David quickly ran out to meet him. Reaching into his shepherd's bag and taking out a stone, he hurled it with his sling and hit the Philistine in the forehead. The stone sank in, and Goliath stumbled and fell face down on the ground. So David triumphed over the Philistine with only a sling and a stone, for he had no sword. Then David ran over and pulled Goliath's sword from its sheath. David used it to kill him and cut off his head.[30]

The fact is David would have remained a shepherd were it not for Goliath. *His victory over the giant was the doorway to his destiny—from shepherd to king.*

Often our challenges and our victory over them define the life we live. Have you ever considered the possibility that God permits the presence of giants and enemies in our lives? The day my wife, Karyn, received the news from her doctor she had an aggressive cancer in her body, she fought. She stood up one Sunday morning and declared to the church congregation, "God did not send this cancer, I have an enemy." There are some fights in our life we did not choose the fight, but we fight anyway. Some fights seem unfair, but the question is, are we going to trust God? Karyn's favourite story through her fight was the story of Shadrach, Meshach, and Abednego, the three Hebrew young men who refused to bow to the king's new idol. They choose to believe God, no matter the outcome.

Daniel 3:17-18 says, "If we are thrown into the blazing furnace, the God whom we serve is able to save us. He will rescue us from your power, Your Majesty. But even if he doesn't, we want to make it clear to you, Your Majesty, that we will never serve your gods or worship the gold statue you have set up." We can trust in God's promises, no matter what it looks like, and believe that He is for us, not against us. His plans are for good, not for evil.

The bigger the giant you defeat, the greater the glory God receives. The process of confronting and overcoming our personal giants actually brings meaning and purpose to our lives. As human beings created in the image of Almighty God,[31] we were never designed to live irrelevant, meaningless lives. To feel that we are is one of the most demoralizing and de-motivating things we can face.

We all desire to make our mark in life, to leave some kind of legacy. I want to see my children and grandchildren planted in the house of God, but I also want to fight for more families and more young people to be planted there. They are worth fighting for and Scripture is clear that there is honour and glory attached to these pursuits. It is God's divine nature to honour those who go the second mile—who give their lives, who face their giants and confront their fears, who fight bravely, armed with His promises.

David had something that to him was worth fighting for. He was promised a reward—riches, a princess, glory—and he responded, "Don't worry about this Philistine, I'll go fight him!" There is something deep within us all that connects with stories of people who overcome adversity. It challenges, encourages, witnesses truth and stirs hope in us.

Take Joshua, another Old Testament hero. God promoted him to lead the Israelites after Moses died.[32] In spite of battles and opposition, Joshua made the stand, saying, "As for me and my house, we will serve the LORD."[33] His biblical account and others like it should stir us to do the same.

A TIME OF CELEBRATION

Serving the Lord is rewarding, but not always easy—sacrifice[34] and "the good fight of faith"[35] are part of the package. David and Joshua were willing to fight, when necessary, to serve God, and their lives were anything but mediocre.

It is a mediocre man who wants the easy way out; God has not called us to live mediocre lives. We say living that way produces peace because we desperately want peace— but peace is not the absence of war; peace is the presence of God. Peace is knowing He is with us in the battles of life.

Many want honour, but are unwilling to sacrifice. Remember, sacrifice means giving up something you value in order to help people. How many women sacrifice their career for their children? How many parents sacrifice to send their kids to college? How many soldiers gave their all for our freedom? How many Christians have sacrificed everything for the benefit of others?

It is the desire of most Christian leaders and many laypeople to bring change, one person at a time. May our churches always love and stand for justice. May we act to bring solutions to problems and declare that we will not accept injustice. May we know and understand the hope of our calling,[36] that when the books are opened in heaven and our names are called,[37] there will be a great and glorious celebration and we will share it with God Almighty for all eternity.

God gave us a glimpse of that celebration in His Word:

Then I heard what sounded like a great multitude, like the roar of rushing waters and like loud peals of thunder, shouting: "Hallelujah! For our Lord God Almighty reigns. Let us rejoice and be glad and give him glory! For the wedding of the Lamb has come, and his bride has made herself ready.

Fine linen, bright and clean, was given her to wear." [Fine linen stands for the righteous acts of the saints.] Then the angel said to me, "Write: 'Blessed are those who are invited to the wedding supper of the Lamb!'" And he added, "These are the true words of God."[38]

The Bride is the Church. Can you picture this scene? Heaven is celebrating. Songs of victory ring out through all the heavens, resonating from the heart of heaven itself: "Hallelujah, Hallelujah, Praise the Lord!"

Here, at the end of the ages, God clothes His Bride, the Church, in the finest linen, an act of honour and reward for her righteous deeds. (Honour is always on the other side of sacrifice, right?) Those who will be at this celebration of all celebrations have not made it because of their works, but by grace in confessing, "Lord Jesus, I believe in You; I accept You into my life; forgive me for all of my sins and mistakes." What a glorious time awaits us!

Thomas Paine, one of the founding fathers of the United States, said, "The harder the conflict, the more glorious the triumph." We who enter into this celebration by God's marvelous grace will experience a time of triumph when He will recognize the righteous deeds of His Church. God himself will remember, reward, and honour all those who have made sacrifices, overcome life's battles and finished their course.[39]

Chapter 8

FIGHTING FULL-ON TO THE FINISH

All endeavour calls for the ability to tramp the last mile, shape the last plan, endure the last hours toil.

The fight to the finish spirit is the one...characteristic we must possess if we are to face the future as finishers.

—*Henry David Thoreau*

There is honour in fighting to the finish, but there is no honour in quitting. Quitting demoralizes the quitter and can effect potentially dangerous consequences to those around. Many stories from Vietnam have been told of new soldiers who became terrified when under heavy fire for the first time. Their orders were to shoot back because their return fire protected their fellow soldiers. If they continued to cower, they exposed the other soldiers with them to death.

Sometimes this cover fire allowed their own men to advance, but doing nothing put everyone in danger. This is called the "fire and manoeuvre" and could be described as the modern-day equivalent to the ancient phalanx and *testudo* techniques.

In Ephesians 6, Paul describes faith as a shield and part of the battle-attire of a believer. In ancient Roman warfare, soldiers would sometimes use a formation called the *tortoise* or the *testudo* (the Latin word for *tortoise*).[1] This required each soldier to interlock their shield with the man beside him, thus not protecting himself but his fellow soldier who fought beside him.

Cassius Dio, a Roman historian who was born around A.D. 165, wrote about the *testudo* when describing the 36 BC campaign of Mark Antony:

"This testudo and the way in which it is formed are as follows. The Baggage animals, the light-armed troops, and the cavalry are placed in the centre of the army. The heavy-armed troops who use the oblong, curved and cylindrical shields are drawn up around the outside, making a rectangular figure, and, facing outward and holding their arms at the ready, they enclose the rest. The others who have flat shields, form a compact body in the centre and raise their shields over the heads of all the others, so that nothing but shields can be seen in every part of the phalanx alike and all the men by the density of the formation are under shelter from missiles. Indeed, it is so marvellously strong that men can walk upon it and whenever they come to a narrow ravine, even horses and vehicles can be driven over it."[2]

If a soldier dropped his shield, he exposed his partner to danger. These highly organized troops would replace exhausted men as they wearied so as to create a perpetual fighting force who would wear down the enemy until they broke the ranks.

The ancient Spartans were similar. They were part of the Greek Empire and were for all intents and purposes a military state. As infants, both male and female were subject to military drill and at the height of its power the Spartan army was among the most feared military force in world history (6th – 4th centuries BC). The attitude of the day was that "one Spartan was worth several men of any other state," due to the fact that "bravery was the ultimate virtue for the Spartans: Spartan mothers would give their sons the shield with the words '[Return] With it or [carried] on it!'...that is to say, either victorious or dead, since in battle, the heavy hoplite shield would be the first thing a fleeing soldier would be tempted to abandon— *rhipsaspia*, 'dropping the shield,' was a synonym for desertion in the field."[3]

One of the popular fighting formations used by the Spartans was the phalanx. The phalanx consisted of each soldier locking shields together, presenting a shield-wall from which protruded a mass of spears. A man who dropped his shield became the weak link and it is believed he was either replaced or killed by his own men in order to sure up the front line. The strength of the phalanx depended on the front line and the front line's success depended on the quick replacement of any fallen soldiers, as any opportunity to breach the line would lead to quick defeat.

This quick study in historical armor not only shows the importance of fighting to the finish; it shows the importance of the shield when in battle. The shield is one of the pieces of spiritual armor that the apostle Paul talked about in Ephesians 6. He told us in that chapter to "put on the whole armor of God,"[4] then he described each piece:

Stand therefore, having girded your waist with truth, having put on the breastplate of righteousness, and having shod your feet with the preparation of the gospel of peace; above all, taking the shield of faith with which you will be able to quench all the fiery darts of the wicked one. And take the helmet of salvation, and the sword of the Spirit, which is the word of God; praying always with all prayer and supplication in the Spirit, being watchful to this end with all perseverance and supplication for all the saints.[5]

It is interesting to note that we are not told to make do with a difficult enemy or situation; we have been given spiritual weapons to maintain "our ground, not yielding or fleeing,"[6] to overcome, to actually walk in victory over the enemy. These weapons have been proven[7]—we've been given the same spiritual armor that Jesus used while He walked among us. If this is His armor, then to the devil, we look like Jesus when we wear it.

Notice too in that passage that a key part of this armor is the shield of faith.[8] We just saw that the shield used by ancient armies was for more than personal defence; it also protected all those around the soldiers. This shows how important it is to be joined together with other believers as we face difficult times.

Some battles are not meant to be fought alone. King Solomon said that two are better than one;[9] Moses said where one can put one thousand to flight, two can put ten thousand to flight.[10] As the shield and battle tactics of ancient soldiers involved protecting fellow soldiers as well as themselves, when Christians fight in spiritual warfare, it is not for ourselves alone but for others, the men and women alongside us. Just as those ancient armies were protected with their physical shields, our faith, like a shield, protects us.

In life we have people who stand with us in our fight for faith. Paul tells us to "Fight the good fight for the true faith. Hold tightly to the eternal life to which God has called you, which you have confessed so well before many witnesses."[11]

People watch our lives. When we quit it sends the message, "If they can't make it, then how can I ever make it?" There is no honour in giving up; however, when we face the battle and overcome it, the result is success. This outlook on life will bring us victory and joy, which are the results of overcoming.

THE JOY OF OVERCOMING

Revelation 2 and 3 mention the person who overcomes four times, followed each time by the bestowing of honour.

He who has an ear, let him hear what the Spirit says to the churches. *To him who overcomes* I will give to eat from the tree of life, which is in the midst of the Paradise of God. He who has an ear, let him hear what the Spirit says to the churches. *He who overcomes* shall not be hurt by the second death. *He who overcomes,* I will make him a pillar in the temple of My God, and he shall go out no more. I will write on him the name of My God and the name of the city of My God, the New Jerusalem, which comes down out of heaven from My God. And I will write on him My new name. *To him who overcomes* I will grant to sit with Me on My throne, as I also overcame and sat down with My Father on His throne.[12]

Imagine the joy at receiving such honour—it's available to all who won't quit. That should be incentive enough to stay in the fight and overcome every battle we face!

Overcoming, quite simply, is a refusal to quit. The dictionary defines *overcome* as conquer, defeat, prevail over (opposition, objectives, temptations). Surmount, overpower, to gain victory; conquer. *Quit* is defined as stop, cease, discontinue, depart, leave, give up, let go, relinquish, resign. Giving up and cowardice (spinelessness), elements of quitting, are aspects of dishonour. Quitting demoralizes the quitter and can effect potentially dangerous consequences to those around.

Ephraim was the second-born son of Joseph and from him was descended Joshua, who became leader of Israel after Moses died.[13] Ephraim also was one of the tribes of Israel who had been prepared with all the other tribes to protect their families and God's people. They were trained to fight, dressed for war, but when the conflict got tough and their brothers needed them, they quit and deserted them on the battlefield.

The warriors of Ephraim, though armed with bows, turned their backs and fled on the day of battle.[14]

Overcoming and honour go hand in hand; so do quitting and dishonour. Although from the time of Moses through to Saul, Ephraim was the most prominent tribe of Israel, they are not found in the book of Revelation when the tribes of Israel are listed around the throne of God.[15] Many honours are conferred on those who refuse to quit and if we refuse to quit we will eventually overcome.

We are called to be overcomers and overcoming requires true strength of character when facing a difficult battle or struggle: The pain of having a child fall away and follow the wrong crowd; overwhelming financial problems, when it seems like everywhere you turn someone wants something from you; the bitterness of divorce and the trauma it causes; the death of a loved one—the list goes on and on. Life is full of challenges, battles we find ourselves in the middle of, often undeserved or without warning. At times we all face the fight against discouragement to keep our hope against the onset of depression. Winners and quitters alike must face battles. Yet, as Ephesians 6 reveals, those of us who are in Christ have been given the weapons we need to overcome the enemy every time. God promises it in His Word: "He shall call upon me, and I will answer him: I will be with him in trouble; I will deliver him, and honour him."[16]

The Hebrew word for *deliver* here means to "equip (for war)... arm for war [as a soldier]."[17] In Christ, then, God equips us to overcome, and we can trust His Word and understand that He will do His part as we do ours. As we serve Him with a thankful heart,

He will carry us through. Watch out that you do not lose what you have worked so hard to achieve. Be diligent so that you receive your full reward.[18]

There is a battle and quitting is not an option.

TAKE YOUR PROMISED LAND!

When the Israelites finally arrived at the Promised Land and the report of giants was given, the people were overcome with fear because of how they saw themselves.[19] They still had the mind-set of slaves despite the fact that they had been set free from slavery forty years beforehand. Thoughts such as *We can't do this! It's too big for us! God has asked something too hard!* would have been rife in the camp.

Today, God has given us one of the greatest tasks in the history of the Church—to preach His Gospel in every nation and after that the end will come.[20]   This could easily be seen as a giant of a task. Many nations—Hindu, Islam, Muslim, Buddhist—are hardened to the Gospel. It would be easy to understand why someone would see this as too hard, too challenging, a too-big-to-conquer giant and their church as too small or weak.

We are called upon by God to rise up and face the enemy; to face life's challenges full-on. God will give us the strength and the grace—He has promised.

He gives power to the weak, and to those who have no might He increases strength. Even the youths shall faint and be weary, and the young men shall utterly fall, but those who wait on the LORD shall renew their strength; they shall mount up with wings like eagles, they shall run and not be weary, they shall walk and not faint.[21]

What does it mean to mount on wings like eagles? "The 'eagles' wings' are figurative," says Keil and Delitzsch in their Bible commentary, "and denote the strong and loving care of God. The eagle watches over its young in the most careful manner, flying under them when it leads them from the nest, least they should fall upon the rocks, and be injured or destroyed."[22] As that passage also indicates, God takes the weary, strengthens them and gives them "support under affliction."[23] So the secret to overcoming is, never quit.

Romans 8:31 says, "What shall we then say to these things? If God be for us, who can be against us?" Quitting isn't an option. Our mandate is to continue with the commission that God has called us to and He is with us to carry us through, even when we're battling giants.

We've talked about giants, but they have a lot to do with overcoming and quitting. A giant is something that stands over us and says, "You won't make it this time. This time I will win and you will die." Giants always try to intimidate us into believing that our problems are bigger than we are.

There were no giants in Egypt when the Israelites were slaves; there were no giants in the wilderness where they wandered and

God changed their attitude from slaves to soldiers. The only place that Israel saw giants was in the Promised Land. What that means for us is this: *the only place we will see a giant in our life as Christians is when we are approaching receiving the promises of God that He has given us.*

So, if you see a giant, congratulations. You are close! Now, keep going and take your Promised Land. Never give up.

Chapter 9

PERSEVERANCE AND HONOUR

Perseverance, dear my lord, keeps honour bright.
—William Shakespeare

Battles are not easy; they are usually fought or won with intense effort and cost, pushing through problems and challenges and refusing to surrender. The quality required to overcome and win the battles in our life is *perseverance*.

Most people who have lived long enough would agree that life gets tough at times, very tough at others. *Perseverance* is the persistence or the tenacity to keep moving forward, especially in the face of adversity.

The word *perseverance* has been defined as being a determined continuation with something or as steady and continued action or belief, usually over a long period and especially despite difficulties or setbacks. For example, we persevere for our family, our faith and our future, despite the problems.

When discussing perseverance, it is important to understand that a tactic of the enemy is to tire us, particularly through tough and challenging times. No doubt that's one of the reasons why the apostle Paul told Timothy, his son in the faith, to "pursue...perseverance."[1]

Earlier, Paul had told the Ephesian believers to pray "always with all prayer and supplication in the Spirit, and watching there unto with all perseverance and supplication for all saints."[2] We've already talked about that verse, but note the word again, *persevere*— to be steadfast, steady, unshakeable.

It is beneficial to be steadfast in our loyalties with our friendships because perseverance doesn't give up when times get tough; it sees things through to their full potential and this includes friendships and relationships. When it comes to our faith, being steadfast means we don't change quickly or unexpectedly. If we are to be predictable, let it be with our faith, our loyalties to God's Church and cause, and to our friends.

Another aspect of perseverance is found in 1 Peter 15–16: "You must be holy in everything you do, just as God who chose you is holy. For the Scriptures say, 'You must be holy because I am holy.'" Holiness depends upon perseverance. *Easton's Illustrated Bible Dictionary* explains, "Personal holiness is a work of gradual development. It is carried on under many hindrances, hence the frequent admonitions to watchfulness, prayer, and perseverance (1 Cor. 1:30; 2 Cor. 7:1; Eph. 4:23, 24)."[3] In his first epistle, Peter counsels perseverance under persecution, connecting this with the practice of living the Christian life.

There are certain non-negotiable areas of one's life that are consistent. History is made, not by those who flow with the ebb and tide of popular opinion, but by those who are steadfast in their convictions, even when that could involve sacrifice and discomfort. What does this mean for you and me? Well, it definitely includes paying attention to the fundamental things such as making the Word of God a priority, reading it and meditating on it daily—because it is like our bread or food.

"People do not live by bread alone, but by every word that comes from the mouth of God."[4]

"Like newborn babies, you must crave pure spiritual milk so that you will grow into a full experience of salvation. Cry out for this nourishment."[5]

[Jesus said,] "I have meat that you know not of."[6]

How can we hope to persevere if we aren't being "fed"? Our energy runs out and we lose our momentum, eventually slowing to a stop and succumbing to defeat. To persevere is to guard the words that proceed from our mouths, to speak words of life in line with God's truth when circumstances are speaking death or loss. To persevere we must encourage ourselves by remembering times past when God has come through in our life or in the lives of others. It means taking responsibility for our spiritual walk and refusing to accept anything that contradicts what God says in His Word.

That all rolls off the tongue so easily and yet it requires a steady and continued action or belief, usually over a long period and especially despite difficulties or setbacks—the very meaning of *perseverance.* Perseverance, then, is a decision, a commitment to continue in our Christian walk, no questions asked—steadfast, steady, unshakeable. Let's look at some historical examples.

AGAINST ALL ODDS

History consistently testifies how its course has been shaped by men and women who, against all odds and though tired to the core, persevered and refused to quit. These were times when the course of history hung in the balance.

In the Middle Ages, the Vikings almost overthrew England. *Guthrum the Viking might have succeeded in conquering all of Wessex if he had not suffered a defeat at the hands of Alfred at the Battle of Edington in 878. At the Battle of Edington, Guthrum's entire army was routed by Alfred's and fled to their encampment where they were besieged by Alfred's fyrd for two weeks.*[7] At the battle of Chalons in 452, Attila the Hun viciously invaded Italy, but at the last minute, Rome was spared. *John Julius Norwich, the historian known for his works on Venice and on Byzantium, said of the battle of Chalons:"It should never be forgotten that in the summer of 451 and again in 452, the whole fate of western civilization hung in the balance. Had the Hunnish army not been halted in these two successive campaigns, had its leader toppled Valentinian from his throne and set up his own capital at Ravenna or Rome, there is little doubt that both Gaul and Italy would have been reduced to spiritual and cultural deserts.*[8]

The Battle of Gettysburg between America's North and South could so easily have been won by the South had they taken control of a small hill called "Little Round Top." Whoever reached this hilltop first had its control and would thereby win the battle. The North beat the South in a footrace up that hill by only a matter of seconds.

Widely recognized as a hero, founding father and first president of the United States of America, George Washington, led the fight for freedom and the birth of a new nation. But if you look a little closer at this great man's life it appears that he was a somewhat reluctant hero. There was a need for someone with experience to step up and lead and Washington's acceptance of this leadership was meeting a need by filling a gap; he was not an ambitious man.

Washington was once defeated in battle and his army dwindled from 30,000 to just 2,400 men. The English were a well-trained, disciplined and provisioned army and for the most part, Washington's men were poor farmers. Underpaid, demoralized and exhausted as his men were, somehow he managed to rally them and continue on.

In 1776 after a humiliating defeat in Brooklyn, New York against the far superior English army, Washington and his men found themselves trapped and surrounded with the Delaware River behind them. Washington called on some fishermen who began to evacuate the wounded first, when divine intervention appeared in the form of a dense fog. Washington seized the opportunity to move his entire army out under the cover of the foggy cloak. But the Delaware was icy, the weather treacherous and the crossing dangerous. Nevertheless, Washington and his 2,400 men made the crossing successfully. The American cause seemed doomed but Washington had formed a daring plan, one that very few people thought could succeed. He would transport his army in boats across the Delaware River for a surprise attack on King George III's hired German soldiers, who were camped in Trenton, New Jersey.

Washington marched his men to Trenton where King George III's hired German soldiers known as the Hessians, had arrived only days earlier to establish their winter quarters. The English objective at all costs was to defeat the uprising for independence and freedom and Washington was considered among the key offenders. Nevertheless the repeatedly-defeated Washington and his army began their march for freedom. Washington's only promise to his men was the chance to get shoes and breakfast at the end of their march. For the most part his soldiers were barefoot, marching through the snow with only the promise of a little relief and comfort when they arrived at Trenton.

Many of the troops did not have boots, so they were forced to wear rags around their feet. Some of the men's feet bled, turning the snow to a dark red. Two men died on the trip.[9] All but these two continued their unbelievable march on Christmas Eve and Christmas Day with the single hope that they could surprise the English. As they marched, Washington rode up and down the line, encouraging the men to continue. General Sullivan sent a courier to tell Washington that the weather was wetting his men's gunpowder. Washington responded, "Tell General Sullivan to use the bayonet. I am resolved to take Trenton."[10]

Arriving mid-morning in Trenton on the December 26, much later than Washington had hoped, his army of nearly exhausted and starving men caught the Hessian army off-guard, defeating them decisively. This victory became a turning-point in the American Revolutionary War, reviving an almost extinct morale or hope for any possibility that freedom was within their sights.

Thomas Paine,[11] who accompanied Washington on the march, wrote, "These are the times that try men's souls." Washington's soldiers were sick, exhausted and malnourished—tried to the very depths of their souls.

What could possibly motivate men like this? Where are such men found?

The fact was they saw something greater than their circumstances and severe hardship. They were fighting for a cause greater than any individual—freedom from the tyranny of the English who were determined to "bind us in all cases whatsoever."[12]

They marched and fought for freedom and the hope of a better future for their children and grandchildren and future generations. There can be no doubt that many of these men would have wanted to give up, some did and some even defected, fighting on the side of the enemy in exchange for food and shoes. Brother who stayed said to brother who left, "You try my soul." It's reminiscent of Esau, who sold his birthright to his brother Jacob to satiate his hunger in exchange for a bowl of soup.[13]

How many times have you been so tired that in some moment in your life you said, "My soul is weary, I cannot go on"? Your soul is squeezed like a vice. Thoughts pull hard on you for the sake of your family, your future, your grandchildren. Wouldn't it just be better for everyone to surrender? Have you ever been there?

Honour is for those who finish, who persevere under the most extreme pressure to quit, who make it to the end. Those who defected or gave up did not share in the glory and honour of Washington's victory at Trenton. Those who endured at great personal cost gained the honour of victory, and their children and grandchildren would later recount the story with pride, how their fathers and grandfathers marched weary to their souls, persevered and overcame, fought and won freedom for their nation.

OUR DECISIONS DEFINE OUR FUTURE

In reflecting on this quality and strength of character, let's turn to God's Word in search of such characteristics in someone. Many accounts of people come to mind, but one that stands out is the story of Ruth.

In the days when the judges ruled in Israel, a severe famine came upon the land. So a man from Bethlehem in Judah left his home and went to live in the country of Moab, taking his wife and two sons with him. The man's name was Elimelech, and his wife was Naomi.[14]

The Moabites were were descendents of Lot (Abraham's nephew) through an incestuous encounter between Lot and his older daughter,[15] and were the enemy of Israel.

[Elimelech and Naomi's] two sons were Mahlon and Kilion. They were Ephrathites from Bethlehem in the land of Judah. And when they reached Moab, they settled there.

Then Elimelech died, and Naomi was left with her two sons. The two sons married Moabite women. One married a woman named Orpah, and the other a woman named Ruth. But about ten years later, both Mahlon and Kilion died. This left Naomi alone, without her two sons or her husband.

Then Naomi heard in Moab that the LORD had blessed his people in Judah by giving them good crops again. So Naomi and her daughters-in-law got ready to leave Moab to return to her homeland. With her two daughters-in-law she set out from the place where she had been living, and they took the road that would lead them back to Judah.

But on the way, Naomi said to her two daughters-in-law, "Go back to your mothers' homes. And may the LORD reward you for your kindness to your husbands and to me. May the LORD bless you with the security of another marriage." Then she kissed them good-bye, and they all broke down and wept.

"No," they said. "We want to go with you to your people."

But Naomi replied, "Why should you go on with me? Can I still give birth to other sons who could grow up to be your husbands? No, my daughters, return to your parents' homes, for I am too old to marry again. And even if it were possible, and I were to get married tonight and bear sons, then what? Would you wait for them to grow up and refuse to marry someone else? No, of course not, my daughters! Things are far more bitter for me than for you, because the LORD himself has raised his fist against me."

And again they wept together, and Orpah kissed her mother-in-law good-bye. But Ruth clung tightly to Naomi. "Look," Naomi said to her, "your sister-in-law has gone back to her people and to her gods. You should do the same."

But Ruth replied, "Don't ask me to leave you and turn back. Wherever you go, I will go; wherever you live, I will live. Your people will be my people, and your God will be my God. Wherever you die, I will die, and there I will be buried. May the LORD punish me severely if I allow anything but death to separate us!" When Naomi saw that Ruth was determined to go with her, she said nothing more.[16]

Picture the difficult predicament in which these three women found themselves. Naomi had two sons who married Moabite women. Naomi's husband died, her sons died and she was left with her two daughters-in-law, who began to follow her as she headed back to Judah; but she had nothing she could offer them—no hope, no future. The daughter-in-law named Orpah left and went back with her family, but Ruth begged Naomi to allow her to remain with her; Naomi finally relented.

It was a tough time for this family. All the men in Naomi's life died, leaving her with no hope for the future, only the prospect to finish her life in poverty. No doubt, she was tired to her soul. Her daughters-in-law had to make a difficult choice—to honour their ex-husbands' family and look after their mother-in-law, or go back to their own families and familiar surroundings.

Our decisions define our future. Those of us who are parents also affect the future of our children by our decisions. It is easy to make the wrong decision because we are tired and worn down. It takes courage, strength of soul, to make the right decision in the face of opposition. But decisions are important. Your life is today what you decided it would be yesterday. If you do not like the life you have, change your decisions. Ruth made a heroic decision, not because of her own need or comforts, but because it was right. Orpah returned to Moab and we do not hear of her again. Ruth became the grandmother of King David. In future generations these descendants would fight against each other —this can be traced back to the decisions these two young women made. Ruth, in an attitude of honour, stayed with her mother-in-law, who had nothing to offer her; but Ruth's decision led to great blessing for generations afterward.

The Moabites were strangers to God; they worshipped idols, false gods. Although Ruth was a Moabite widow, she did not look out for her own life but chose to be with Naomi—her motive was to serve. She came with nothing to a foreign country and as a foreigner she was not permitted to work in the harvest. She could only glean from the leftovers after the harvesters had finished. Yet despite such overwhelming adversity, Ruth ended up blessed in marriage to Boaz (a wealthy, virtuous and honourable kinsman of Naomi's) and in the lineage of Jesus Christ.

Decisions we may make in a matter of seconds can determine the course of our life. Orpah chose comfort. Be careful with the decisions you make when you are tired or in a crisis—the temptation to abandon everything will be strong.

COMFORT, PROTECTION, WISDOM AND STRENGTH

"He will speak out against the Most High and wear down the saints of the Highest One, and he will intend to make alterations in times and in law; and they will be given into his hand for a time, times, and half a time."[17]

This passage from the book of Daniel identifies one of the goals of the enemy that was mentioned earlier—to make us tired and feel, "I can't do it anymore, I can't possibly keep going." Wearing us down is the enemy's tactic; Daniel spoke of it and so did Moses. In Deuteronomy 25:18, Moses said that the enemy always attacks the weak; so wherever we are weak he will target his attacks. It is very important that we understand his strategy because for the sake of our children and our future, we must never quit. The decisions we make are critical at times like those. We must be on our guard and determine in our hearts that no matter how difficult things become, we will persevere and keep going. Of course life has times of challenge and hardship, trials and difficulties, but the Word of God teaches us to run to Him, never from Him because He is our comfort and protection, our wisdom and our strength.

> The name of the LORD is a strong tower; the righteous run to it and are safe.[18]

> Have you never heard? Have you never understood? The LORD is the everlasting God, the Creator of all the earth. He never grows weak or weary. No one can measure the depths of his understanding.

> He gives power to the weak and strength to the powerless. Even youths will become weak and tired, and young men will fall in exhaustion. But those who trust in the LORD will find new strength. They will soar high on wings like eagles. They will run and not grow weary. They will walk and not faint.[19]

What a beautiful promise. When you are tired, God is there. If you persevere and continue forward doing what is right, His promise to you is that He will give you new strength!

> Let us not become weary in doing good, for at the proper time we will reap a harvest if we do not give up.[20]

> The storm will pass, but God is eternal.

Chapter 10

WHAT'S IN A NAME

We make men without chests and expect of them virtue and enterprise.
We laugh at honour and are shocked to find traitors in our midst. We castrate and bid the geldings to be fruitful.

—*C.S. Lewis*

Once upon a time, a person's reputation was a thing of value. Can you remember when the word of a man or woman had weight?

Sadly, the younger generation cannot recall such a time for the most part, but I can assure you there was a period in my lifetime when you could leave the door to your home open when you went out, when locking your car was an uncommon practice and no one would even entertain the idea of taking anything—everything would still be in your car or your home when you returned. A code of honour existed that said, "I will not take anything that is not mine."

These days it seems those values are taken lightly and have all but disappeared.

Of course, some still care about these things, but the tide has turned and to increasing numbers of people, such values belong to a bygone era; they are no longer relevant.

Think about that for a moment—something of intense value has been thrown away in exchange for something worthless. We have lost a part of our humanity and now find ourselves living in a world that is increasingly hostile and unsafe. Why would we as a society do such an obviously foolish thing? Many of us didn't value trust; we bought the lie that we must "look out for No.1" and that it's "every man for himself."

Have you ever watched one of those old black and white movies where a man who felt his reputation had been damaged would challenge the offender to a duel? The idea was that a man's reputation was worth defending, even to death. Such things can seem a little barbaric in today's world, but it shows what was of value in that era.

One particular era when it was extremely important to defend honour was in the days of King Arthur. The story of King Arthur and the Knights of the Round Table is legendary. Great mystery and controversy surround these characters, but it is believed historically that they lived in the period at the beginning of the fall of the great Roman Empire, when it was losing its grip on Great Britain while at the same time Britain's tribes were divided and fighting amongst themselves.[1]

The legend tells of Arthur's champions, the Knights of the Round Table, among whom was the most skilled knight of all, Lancelot. A large number of historic and poetic accounts of Lancelot describe him as greatly desired by the ladies and pursued by a number of them. One source described his adulterous indiscretions, saying: "Legend also says that Lancelot was the father of Galahad by Elaine. It was another Elaine, Elaine of Astolat, who died of a broken heart because Lancelot did not return her love and affection.

"Many sources tell us of the love shared toward each other of Lancelot and Queen Guinevere. There may be some truth to this since Lancelot was a favorite of the Queen's, and he rescued her from the stake on two different occasions."[2]

Lancelot was infamous for his affair with King Arthur's wife Guinevere. Arthur's other loyal knights learned of Lancelot's dishonour and informed the king.

"Lancelot had one failing, his adulterous love of Queen Guinevere. They tried to keep this love secret, it became known, and eventually brought about the undoing of the Round Table.

"Lancelot and Guinevere's love for each other grew slowly. Initially Guinevere kept Lancelot away from her. Eventually, however the pair became lovers. Sir Meliagaunt grew suspicious and confronted Sir Lancelot in front of both the king and queen. The 'insult' led to single combat between the two, in order to reveal the truth. Sir Lancelot overpowered Sir Meliagaunt, and cleaved his head into two bits. Sir Lancelot and Queen Guinevere's honour were restored.

"Sir Meliagaunt was not the only knight suspicious of the pair's relationship. Sir Agravain and Sir Modred, King Arthur's nephew, led a band of 12 knights to Guinevere's chamber where they disturbed the lovers in bed. Sir Lancelot effected his escape by fighting his way out of the castle, but Guinevere was seized and condemned to burn to death for her adultery. Sir Lancelot returned several days later to rescue his Guinevere, killing several of King Arthur's knights in the process. King Arthur later attacked Lancelot's castle without success."[3]

When Lancelot was confronted, he fought each of his accusers in defence of his honour. At this he felt his honour was justified—the idea was that "might makes right."

Nowadays there are those who think that because they are stronger, they have certain rights—a man who abuses a woman just because he can; the strong taking advantage of the weak just because they can. Here is the question: Does might make right? Was Lancelot justified in his affair with Guinevere and dishonour of King Arthur because he could defeat the other knights or because of his superior bravery and swordsmanship?

Knights were also known as gentlemen and they would vow or pledge to defend their king and the kingdom with their strength. The penalty for breaking these vows was death. They were thought of as *chivalrous*—"marked by honour, generosity...courtesy...and high-minded consideration especially to women."[4]

Historically, when Christianity was young, chivalry was common. A gentleman's word carried weight; yes meant yes and no meant no. Words had value. Times have changed, even in the church.

How uncommon but refreshing these days to find people who mean exactly what they say; their word carries weight. By contrast, the norm today seems to be that a person's yes may mean yes, or they could be playing a definition game in their mind. I remember a politician saying one time, "It depends on what the meaning of the word is, is."

In the days of our grandparents, a handshake was as good as one's word. To many, such a gesture was indeed more binding and of greater value than a signature; the word carried weight. Now we need contracts, legal documents and terminology simply because people don't keep their word anymore. We engage attorneys to explain the terminology and implications of legally binding contracts. We have gone from being the "head" to becoming the "tail" instead;[5] from being in control to being controlled. What does "is" mean? Yes doesn't necessarily mean yes and no isn't even no anymore.

As confessing followers of Jesus Christ, our word should all the more carry weight. People will watch us and the integrity, or lack of integrity, of what we say and will be either attracted to Christ or repelled by it. One of the most common excuses or complaints heard from unsaved people concerning Christians is that they are a bunch of hypocrites or they don't practice what they preach. In other words, they say one thing but live another. The value and weight of the words we say are so vitally important. It comes down to making the decision to do what we say; otherwise, don't say it. Let our yes be yes and our no, no. We are living epistles, read by all men.[6]

HONOUR YOUR WORD

In his book *Maximized Manhood,*[7] Dr. Edwin Louis Cole taught that we are created in God's image and likeness and so when people look at our lives they should be able to see His image in us; we should be like Him.

In Psalm 138:2 we see a particular character trait of God—a principle concerning who He is:

> I will worship toward Your holy temple and praise Your name for Your loving-kindness and for Your truth and faithfulness; for You have exalted above all else Your name and Your word and You have magnified Your word above all Your name![8]

God is saying that He has placed His Word even above His name!

Therefore, God elevated him to the place of highest honour and gave him the name above all other names, that at the name of Jesus every knee should bow, in heaven and on earth and under the earth, and every tongue confess that Jesus Christ is Lord, to the glory of God the Father.[9]

Jesus has been given a name which is above every other name anywhere in any time in any place, ultimate authority under which every living thing will bow, and yet... the one thing which God has placed above His all powerful, wonderful name is His Word. How can this be? God is showing us something about himself and therefore about ourselves as creatures uniquely made in His image and likeness[10]—our name is as good as our word.

In marriage and family, for example, the greatest gift a man can give is a good name. The greatest thing a wife gives her husband is trust. How many men will say to their wives, "Just trust me," but to a woman, trust is earned. When a man gives a woman his word, if she believes his word, she receives his word. But when a woman marries, she receives her husband's name as well. He may give her his name, but his name is worth only as much as his word.

There are too many who, after they marry, make promises but don't keep their word. A husband may promise to take his wife out to a nice dinner, for example, but as the time approaches his friends call and he decides to go out with them instead, so he'll make some kind of excuse to his wife. Little by little his word loses weight and soon his word will not even be believable. When our word loses its value so does our name. Sadly, in time she will become embarrassed by the name she carries, causing her to feel demoralized and resentful.

Today, when you hear the name Tiger Woods, what is your first thought. Great athlete? Champion golfer? Moral failure? He was the one man who could make television ratings go up on a PGA tour. His name was weighty, sponsors paid millions to use his influence to sell their product. He was the one you looked for on the golf course, even if you don't understand the game, his name made you stop and see what he was up to. Then, his private life came to light. A fall, his word to his wife violated, his name, well, damaged. What you do in private, eventually will come to light publicly. Often people think their private life will not effect their public life, but what is done in private eventually will be seen in public. The sponsors who paid so highly for his name on their product were gone. His private life cost him millions. His name lost value.

There are other names we could remember—Presidents Richard Nixon or Bill Clinton. Other great athletes like Michael Vick or Barry Bonds. In the Bible, think of Adam, Sampson, King David —there was a time each of their names was tarnished because of a mistake, a moral failure, but there also was a time of restoration. Though bad decisions have created chaos in many lives, a turning back to God, a time of reflection and change of heart is the doorway to restoring what was lost. A good name can be restored. Samson had one final great victory, King David's throne was established with honour again. You don't need to be remembered by yesterday's failure, begin to honour your word today, and your name will carry weight again.

What do people think when they hear your name? What thoughts or words do they associate with you? "He's a good man." "She's a devoted wife." "He says one thing but does another." "She always wants something from people." What do you want people to say about you? If you aren't already, start to be that person.

Remember, a name is only as good as the person's word. God desires that our word would carry weight—He wants us to be honourable with our words and give weight to them. Make the decision that you always will honour your word. At times it may cost a lot and even be to your own hurt, but no matter what, keep your word. It will mean you will have to become very intentional in giving your word, but it is so worth it. The value of your name will grow and people will begin to trust you with more and more.

Proverbs 22:1 says, "Choose a good reputation over great riches; being held in high esteem is better than silver or gold." Does your family trust your word? Are your promises valued? Give your children a name they will be proud to carry to the next generation. How tragic when children are embarrassed by their parent; by the name they carry because their father took his word and his responsibility as a father lightly. That's not the way it's supposed to be.

A good name is more valuable than gold, so if your name isn't a good name right now, decide to turn that around beginning today. Make the decisions that will earn you back a good name and become known as a person of your word. When you honour God in word and deed, it will cause you to guard your tongue and to do what you promise. Not only will you earn a good name, but a reputation of being a person with character.

Chapter 11

FACING OFF

Character is what you are in the dark.

—*D.L. Moody*

There is a saying that goes, "The oil always rises to the top." It basically means that whatever is hidden will eventually rise to the surface. Character, or a lack of it, reacts the same way.

Some people have the appearance of being "big," but if there is a lack of character in them—a lack of integrity or inner strength—sooner or later it will become evident in their lives. Proverbs 23:7 says, "For as [a man] thinks in his heart, so is he."[1] Another way of saying this is that what a man believes, is where he'll end up.

A good person produces good things from the treasury of a good heart, and an evil person produces evil things from the treasury of an evil heart. What you say flows from what is in your heart.[2]

It matters what is hidden inside us because at some point it will eventually surface in our lives since it is a part of who we are internally. God wants us big on the inside because then we will be able to handle the tests and trials of life and not be taken out by them. That inner "bigness" comes from our relationship with the Lord—spending time daily in His presence, in His Word and in prayer.

David in the Bible is a good example. As a young boy David tended his father's sheep. He often spent long periods of time out in the mountains and valleys alone with the flock—and with God. While there, David built a relationship with the Lord, praying and conversing with Him, and worshiping and singing praises to Him—things that helped develop David's character. That was evident when a prophet came to his town, sent by God to find the next king of Israel.

> The LORD said to Samuel, "Don't judge by his appearance or height, for I have rejected him. The LORD doesn't see things the way you see them. People judge by outward appearance, *but the LORD looks at the heart.*[3]

In this scripture the prophet Samuel was looking at which of Jesse's eight sons he was to anoint as king. The first seven each seemed a viable choice, but God rejected them and led Samuel to anoint David, the youngest son, as king of Israel because God was looking at what was in David's heart. Most people assess or make judgements on others based on what they see, but God deals with us inside; in our hearts.

Heart has been defined as "one's innermost *character*, feelings, or inclinations."[4] It is our moral fiber. Character traits can be good or bad—good traits include being compassionate, forgiving, obedient, diligent, generous, trustworthy, and persevering, among others; bad traits are just the opposite. The fact is that character, or heart, is indispensable for building our own lives and making a difference in the lives of others.

There are things in life that we must fight for or we will lose: fighting for our marriage, fighting for our children, fighting the good fight of faith[5] and fighting to see people delivered from the wages of sin[6] and the bondages that entangle them. We must continue the fight, not for the love of it (although I think there are those who enjoy a good fight!), but for what is worth saving. Developing good character traits will help us to continue the fight until we win.

FACING OFF

Chapter 7 of the book of Daniel recounts a prophetic dream that Daniel had concerning four kingdoms and the coming of the Lord. Daniel saw four beasts in that dream that are symbolic of those four monarchies. As the dream unfolds, something interesting is revealed to Daniel about them: "The 'beasts' here represent the world powers, in their beast-like, grovelling character";[7] in other words, they lacked character.

Earlier, during the first year of King Belshazzar's reign in Babylon, Daniel had a dream and saw visions as he lay in his bed. He wrote down the dream, and this is what he saw.

In my vision that night, I, Daniel, saw a great storm churning the surface of a great sea, with strong winds blowing from every direction. Then four huge beasts came up out of the water, each different from the others.

The first beast was like a lion with eagles' wings. As I watched, its wings were pulled off, and it was left standing with its two hind feet on the ground, like a human being. And it was given a human mind.

Then I saw a second beast, and it looked like a bear. It was rearing up on one side, and it had three ribs in its mouth between its teeth. And I heard a voice saying to it, "Get up! Devour the flesh of many people!"

Then the third of these strange beasts appeared, and it looked like a leopard. It had four bird's wings on its back, and it had four heads. Great authority was given to this beast.

Then in my vision that night, I saw a fourth beast—terrifying, dreadful, and very strong. It devoured and crushed its victims with huge iron teeth and trampled their remains beneath its feet. It was different from any of the other beasts, and it had ten horns.[8]

Daniel's dream speaks of four beasts coming out from the sea. As the passage reveals, the first beast in his dream is a lion, the second a bear, the third a leopard and the fourth beast did not resemble anything; it was like a monster. We know that these four beasts are four kingdoms, and we know that it is a prophecy of the coming of Jesus Christ. The lion represented the Babylonian kingdom, the bear was the Medes and Persian kingdom, the leopard was the Grecian kingdom; the fourth beast was the Roman Empire, which historically is when Jesus Christ, the Messiah, was born and lived on earth.

In fact, this portion of scripture is why the people of New Testament times were aware of the imminent arrival of the Messiah. The time the disciples of John the Baptist came and asked Jesus whether He was the One who was to come or if they were to wait for someone else shows that people of this day knew to be looking for and were awaiting the Messiah.[9]

In Daniel's prophetic dream, something unusual happens toward the end of the fourth kingdom. He tells of seeing a "little horn" that spoke of great things:

> As I was looking at the horns, *suddenly another small horn appeared among them.* Three of the first horns were torn out by the roots to make room for it. This little horn had eyes like human eyes and a mouth that was boasting arrogantly.[10]

As Daniel saw this vision, he focused on the fourth beast and specifically on the ten horns, and then gave special attention to the little horn that suddenly appeared. It's as though everything else he was describing in the vision was leading up to this specific thing. It caught Daniel's attention because this smaller horn seemed to become bigger than the other ten and it began to speak accusations and insolences against the One who is seated on the throne.

Then in Daniel 7:21, Daniel says something that, at first, is very disturbing:

"As I watched, this horn was waging war against the saints and defeating them."

How is it possible that this horn was waging war against Christians, and was winning? When we become Christians, it's not long before we find out that we have an adversary. Remember, we are in a battle and the enemy is the devil. So why is the devil so intent on facing off against us?

To bring some perspective here we need to understand that there will be times in our lives when, for all intents and purposes, it seems as though the enemy is winning the fight against us. What we need to realize in the face of this "little horn" that looms so large in our lives and which has been the focus of this book is that honour and reward are on the other side of sacrifice; victory is on the other side of the battle.

THE JUDGE WILL SIT

Looking further into Daniel 7, we see the edge we have over the adversary.

"Until the Ancient of Days came and pronounced judgment in favor of the saints of the Most High, and the time came when they possessed the kingdom."[11]

Judgement was made in favor of the saints when the "Ancient of Days came." This is one of my favorite names of Jesus in the Bible—it literally means "He who is older than days." It is the same name as in John 1:1 which says, "In the beginning was the Word."[12] The beginning is found in Genesis chapter 1, "in the beginning God," one of His first creations was time. Genesis 1:3-5 says,

> Then God said, "Let there be light," and there was light.
>
> And God saw that the light was good. Then he separated the light from the darkness.
>
> God called the light "day" and the darkness "night." And evening passed and morning came, marking the first day.

Notice the words, "the first day". Time started. Before the first day, we have eternity. After the last day, we will have eternity. From the first day to the last day, we have time. We are limited by time, we move minute to minute, hour to hour, day to day throughout time until that day when we will see Christ face to face. So for us, time is a limitation, but God is eternal. There are no limitations on His existence. Before the first day, He existed, He was. The same is true of the Ancient of days, on the first day, He was Ancient. He is without time or limit – He is eternal – without origin or end. He is perennial, interminable and innascible (not subject to birth; self-existent). The beginning was the first day and at the first day, He already was—He was ancient on the first day!

But here is something that seems baffling:

Thrones were set up while I was watching, and the Eternal God took his place. His clothing and his hair were white as snow. His throne was a blazing fire with fiery wheels, and flames were dashing out from all around him. Countless thousands were standing there to serve him.

The time of judgment began, and the books were opened. I watched closely to see what would happen to this smaller horn because of the arrogant things it was saying. Then before my very eyes, the fourth beast was killed and its body destroyed by fire. The other three beasts had their authority taken from them, but they were allowed to live a while longer.[13]

The vision was of beasts, the fourth beast, ten horns and little horn which spoke insolent words— rude, disrespectful, contemptuous, insulting, excessive, arrogant words. A bad character trait for sure!

But did you notice something? In Daniel's vision, all of this occurs before the throne of God where the weight of His presence is, where His glory is, where His throne is—the throne of the One who rules the universe and all creation, where the King of kings is seated! There's a reason why that is an important point. Whenever anyone in the Bible saw the throne of God, they fell as though dead.[14]

When Isaiah saw God's throne, he cried, "I am undone![15] When the apostle John received the book of Revelation as a vision on the island of Patmos, he wrote about his reaction to seeing "someone like the Son of Man" in Revelation 1:17, saying, "When I saw him, I fell at his feet as if I were dead. But he laid his right hand on me and said, 'Don't be afraid! I am the First and the Last.'"

In the context of Daniel 7, he says in verse 11, "I watched closely to see what would happen to this smaller horn because of the arrogant things it was saying." Now notice this: In the midst of the glorious presence of God where angels worship, seraphim shout "Holy! Holy! Holy!"[16] and where His glory abides, this "horn" continued to speak profanities and what's more, refused to stop! It kept on in the very presence of God and His throne.

> He will speak against the Most High and oppress his saints and try to change the set times and the laws. The saints will be handed over to him for a time, times and half a time.[17]

This little horn is the spirit of antichrist. That term refers to anyone "who is against Christ, or opposes himself to him; as he who denies his sonship, his deity, his humanity, his offices, and his grace, manifestly does."[18] To understand this better, let's look briefly at the context of the whole of scripture in Daniel 7.

> This spirit of antichrist has been with mankind since the very beginning. In the Garden of Eden, satan (in the form of a serpent) told the woman, "You won't die!… God knows that your eyes will be opened as soon as you eat it, and you will be like God, knowing both good and evil."[19]

Second Thessalonians 2:4 says that the objective of the antichrist is to sit in God's temple as God.

> He will exalt himself and defy everything that people call god and every object of worship. He will even sit in the temple of God, claiming that he himself is God.

In 1 John 2:18, John said that this spirit is in the world today. This was the same spirit that tempted Jesus in the wilderness trying to persuade Him to bow down and worship it.[20] This has been the desire of Lucifer from his origins in heaven before his fall,[21] and, in fact, was the very reason for it.

> You said in your heart, I will ascend to heaven; I will exalt my throne above the stars of God; I will sit upon the mount of assembly in the uttermost north. I will ascend above the heights of the clouds; I will make myself like the Most High.[22]

Before the foundation of the world, God resisted satan, casting him out from His presence. Satan ended up on the earth and his only hope was to terminate the Seed—God's promise to redeem mankind from the fall. At the cross, as Jesus hung naked, beaten, bleeding, dying and at the point of death, it appeared as though satan was going to succeed. When Jesus died and was entombed, things looked very bleak indeed. But the judgement sat. That is a legal term as when a judge strikes his gavel on the podium—the judge speaks and the ruling is made—the matter is decided and the case closed, no longer subject to further deliberation.

God gave His judgement on Jesus and He rose from the dead!

Satan's act of treason, luring Adam's wife into sin with the bait "You can be like God" is the very same spirit that tempted Jesus. Today this spirit of antichrist wars against the saints, God's people, because satan knows his time is running out and the heat is on. When he challenged God the Father, he was cast out of heaven. When he challenged the Son of God, Jesus was raised from the dead.[23] In these times in which we live, satan is attempting desperately to delay his final judgement. Revelation 12:12 says,

> Therefore, rejoice, O heavens! And you who live in the heavens, rejoice! But terror will come on the earth and the sea, for the devil has come down to you in great anger, knowing that he has little time.

Notice again, the devil knows he has little time. His only way to delay the final judgement, is to make war against all who keep God's commandments and maintain their testimony for Jesus.

So, satan knows his time is short, his only hope is to delay the day of judgement. How? By making war against you. He will try to tire you, to discourage you, to wear you out.

So how do we win? Revelation 12:11 says, "And they have defeated him by the blood of the Lamb and by their testimony. And they did not love their lives so much that they were afraid to die."

Two things are mentioned here, Christ's sacrifice, and our testimony. That is how we win. Christ made a way for us to win at the cross. How many lives have been changed by that cross, that is our power. There may be a lot I don't know but I do know He has changed me, and no one can take that away. No one can argue away someone's personal experience, so when we feel tired, discouraged, like life is too hard, remember this saying... when the devil reminds you of your past failures, remind him of his future.

Then the devil, who had deceived them, was thrown into the fiery lake of burning sulfur, joining the beast and the false prophet. There they will be tormented day and night forever and ever.[24]

A day of final judgement is coming not only for mankind,[25] but for satan as well—and satan's only leverage is to try to delay it. Again, it will appear as though he will succeed for a time, but it is written that at halftime, the Judge will sit and victory shall be awarded to His people.

Victory is always on the other side of the battle.

CONQUERING THE KINGS

On the level of our own lives here and now, how does this "little horn" fight against us? In Daniel 7:25 you may recall that satan oppresses the saints. Literally, "He shall speak great words against the most High, and shall wear out the saints of the most High."[26] His goal is to wear us out; to tire us, get us to give up, to quit. We've talked about that before, but it is important to mention it again to remind you that there will be times in life when it will appear as though the enemy is succeeding and your problem will *seem* to be much larger than it is—too big even for God to handle.

When Joshua replaced Moses as leader of God's people after Moses had died, God gave him a promise, the same promise that He gave Moses.

"Wherever you set foot, you will be on land I have given you... no one will be able to stand against you as long as you live. For I will be with you as I was with Moses. I will not fail you or abandon you."[27]

God didn't mention that the fulfilment of this promise involved conquering over thirty kings.[28] The fact is when God gives us territory, it means that territory is taken from the enemy. God did counsel Joshua several times to "be strong and very courageous."[29] The enemy will fight us, especially at those times—he's not just going to roll out the red carpet and say, "Oh hey! God said you can have my territory? No problem, I'll just leave and you can have it!" I don't think so!

The truth is that in following Christ and seeing His promises fulfilled in our lives, we have an enemy who is trying with all his might to delay the inevitable—his defeat. The thing we should keep in the front of our mind always is that God has already given us the victory over him, but there is a process of "conquering the kings" on the journey there. The question isn't, "Will there be a fight?" The question is, "Are you up for the fight?"

Keep in mind that Ephesians 6:10–18 gives us a full description of how to fight the enemy. If we focus on fighting people, then our focus is misplaced. The Word of God instructs us clearly, leaving us with no doubt that "our struggle is not against flesh and blood, but against the rulers, against the authorities, against the powers of this dark world and against the spiritual forces of evil in the heavenly realms."[30]

Refuse to give the enemy any advantage. Satan has no authority over us as believers unless we give it to him, so do not give him any! Cut off all his angles and put on your spiritual armor.

Yes, it will cost us something to stand in the face of the enemy, when it seems as though all is lost, but having done all—*stand!*[31] The cost of conquering is always worth it because God is absolutely faithful and true to His Word and will be with us through whatever we face.

Remember this: The Ancient of Days *will* prevail; the judgement from the throne is sure and has already been determined. So be encouraged to never give up. It's not easy sometimes—but we all have to make the same kind of choices in our lives not to quit. Thank God we have the knowledge of the ending and that the judgement is secured. Fix your heart, your hope and confidence in this and never forget that honour is on the other side of sacrifice and victory is at the other side of the fight.

When you feel as though you are at the end of your strength to go on, do what I did the last time I went to climb Machu Picchu in Peru—take one step at a time. Climbing that mountain meant I had to conquer it. I had been there many times before and had made it to the top, but somehow after reaching the age of fifty, it seemed so much harder and it sure wasn't fun anymore! Although I felt exhausted, I brought it right back to this one thing—just keep putting one foot in front of the other, one step at a time. Keep going until you get there. That's what I did on that mountain, and I made it, I'm happy to report. You can make it too on whatever mountain of difficulty you encounter.

This is a life principle and when we apply it to our lives, it will cause us to overcome every kind of opposition and challenge that tries to take us out.

The day will come when the Ancient of Days will declare *"Enough!"* Judgement shall sit. Victory will be awarded, to you and to me. In fact, it's not a matter of waiting until then to defeat the enemy of our soul—walking with Christ one day at a time will always lead us into victory; that is His promise.[32]

> For God is not unjust. He will not forget how hard you have worked for him and how you have shown your love to him by caring for other believers, as you still do. Our great desire is that you will keep on loving others as long as life lasts, in order to make certain that what you hope for will come true. Then you will not become spiritually dull and indifferent. Instead, you will follow the example of those who are going to inherit God's promises because of their faith and endurance.[33]

> So let's not get tired of doing what is good. At just the right time we will reap a harvest of blessing if we don't give up.[34]

God will remember. Honour will be given.

Chapter 12

HOW DO WE HONOUR?

A man who honours God privately will show it by making good decisions publicly.

—*Ed Cole*

Gratitude confirms relationships. In December of 1998, my friend and mentor, John Maxwell, suffered a heart attack. Two medical doctors, John Bright Cage and Jeff Marshall, had made a promise to Dr. Maxwell, *we will take care of you*. So when John Maxwell had his medical emergency, he was met at the hospital and comforted with these words, "We are here to take care of you, everything's going to be fine."

Ten years later, John Maxwell wanted to show gratitude to these doctors for saving his life. He took them to a fine restaurant, and during the dinner engagement, read to them the following letter...

Doctors John Bright Cage and Jeff Marshall,
12/4/08

Ten years ago I had a heart attack. God used both of you to spare my life. This is a letter of gratitude. The words in this letter are from my heart. They must be written as a tangible way of giving thanks to you. I believe that silent gratitude isn't much good to anyone.

Your lives have been dedicated to helping people. No doubt over the years many have been given a second chance to live. For 10 years I have been living my "second-chance" life. Because of God's goodness and your giftedness, allow me to briefly share what has happened during this time:

- I have enjoyed my extra 10 years with Margaret and my family.

- Five grandchildren have been born and stolen my heart.

- 38 books have been written that have sold over 15 million copies.

- Amazon.com inducted me into their Hall of Fame.

- I have been named the "World's #1 Leadership Guru".

- 3 Leadership events have been founded by me:

Catalyst – A young leader's conference averages 12,000 per event.

Maximum Impact Simulcast reaches 100,000 people each year.

Exchange is a high level executive experience.

- Two of my companies have experienced wonderful growth:

INJOY Stewardship Services has partnered with 4,000 churches and raised over $4 billion.

EQUIP has trained 3 million leaders in 113 countries.

- It has been my privilege to speak for the United Nations, West Point, NASA, CIA and many Fortune 500 companies.

• Most important, over 7,500 people have received Christ through my teaching!

1 Samuel 2:9 says, "God protectively cares for his faithful friends, step by step." Dr. Cage it was no "accident" when you handed me your business card and said, "John, God has asked me to take care of you. Call me at anytime if you need help." Dr. Marshall, it was no "accident" that you met me at the hospital with your team and said, "We are here to take care of you, everything's going to be fine."

For the last 10 years I have continually expressed to God my gratefulness for both of you. Tonight I give you this letter and say with great love and appreciation, "Thank you!"

Your friend,

John Maxwell

To show honour often is a simple—"thank you." Gratitude.

A friend of mine who actually helped in researching many of the stories in this book is Lieutenant Colonel Randy Eims. I knew he served in the US Army and even commanded men who are Medal of Honor recipients. So to be accurate in my research, I asked him about the honours he received while serving, here is the e-mail he sent back...

I retired a Lieutenant Colonel, Infantry, US Army, served in Vietnam in 1969, 71 and 72 with the 101st Airborne Division and later during Desert Storm. Twenty-nine and one half years of service that included combat command

and combat operations ready units in Europe, the US and Asia. A paratrooper, decorated for valor in combat with over 30 awards to include three Legions of Merit, Bronze Stars, Air Medal, Joint awards, the Combat Infantry Badge, Joint Chiefs of Staff badge, numerous foreign combat awards and unit citations.

I was humbled by Randy's service. He never talks about this, I was actually surprised he told me this much. Today he is a humble servant, who loves his grandchildren and serving in his church. You would never know the extent of his meritorious military service. I simply responded with the words, "Thank you for serving."

Here is his response to my thank you...

Professional soldiers are hesitant to relate any awards. They normally sardonically remark, "all of those and $2.50 will get you a cup of coffee." I may have passed on to you one of my favorite quotes by Calvin Coolidge "No person was ever honoured for what he received. Honour has been the reward for what he gave." I rarely reflect that much on my experiences in the Army and combat. Thanks for that opportunity, although but momentarily. I would give it all to preach one sermon with the power and anointing of a Robert Barriger sermon. Just an aside, after all those years as a soldier.

Wow, thank you Randy Eims for serving, and thank you to all who have served and sacrificed to make our country free.

I admire those who serve, be it in military service, public service, or social service. Remember Churchill's words, "a nation that fails to honour its heroes, will soon have no heroes to honour." In society today, we need heroes, real, reproducible heroes. Heroes that we can hear our children say,"when I grow up, I want to be just like..." What you honour in your life, you produce.

How do we honour, say thank you? When you see the uniform, say thanks, buy them their Starbucks in line, pay their restaurant bill, or just walk up and say it—Thank you for serving.

A friend recently told me the story of a man he was considering hiring for an important position to represent a large ministry. The job involved travel, liaising with other leaders as well as teaching biblical principles. On one particular occasion when my friend was having lunch with this potential employee, the man spoke roughly to the waitress, treating her disrespectfully. Immediately my friend realized that this was not the man for the job and in his mind promptly dismissed him as a candidate.

The focus of this book has been the nature, power, cost, and rewards of honour, and that story illustrates one of the main points— honour (and dishonour) is shown in the way we treat others. Honour is given through our words and our actions, in our impartiality and in the giving of grace and kindness to the people we meet and do life with. Honour is not prejudiced or partial or based on what benefit we may or may not receive by the giving of it.

Here's another point: just as we can't demand loyalty from someone, we can't demand honour. Honour can be taught, even required, where it is due and deserved, but where honour is not deserved, yet forcefully required, it becomes abusive. For the most part, though, honour is an attitude of the heart. It is a show of respect; it can be a reward.

We've seen that there are two kinds of honour: public and private. *Private honour* deals with purity, values and laurels; a sense of pride when we know we've done something good or right. Remember David, the shepherd boy who killed a giant and became a king? He found courage to kill the giant, Goliath, publicly because he first had private victory. Before the giant, David had killed a lion and a bear while shepherding his sheep.[1] In other words, we should be diligent to guard our honour in private, as private philosophy determines public performance.

Remember Haman, Mordecai and Esther? Haman sought honour he didn't deserve. He lusted for recognition and the applause of men and was willing to steal it; he had no private ethics, morals, or character, he cared only for himself. On the other hand, with the help of Esther, Mordecai was able to save the Jewish people from annihilation. Mordecai cared for his people at the risk of his own welfare and that of Esther, whom he loved like a daughter. Esther loved her uncle and her people but esteemed her husband the king. Both Mordecai and Esther privately acted honourably at great personal risk and were publically honoured as a result. Haman, who acted dishonourably, ended up hanging from the gallows he had constructed for Mordecai's demise.

Public honour is an open show of respect and reward for something deserved. God honours publicly those who honour Him privately. Let's look at a couple examples in the Bible.

Luke 7:36–49 tells how Jesus was a guest in the home of Simon the Pharisee when a "sinful woman" began to wash Jesus' feet with her tears. Then she wiped them with her hair and anointed them with perfume. Jesus taught from her example: "Therefore, I tell you, her many sins have been forgiven—as her great love has shown. But whoever has been forgiven little loves little."[2]

The passage in Matthew 26:6–13 is another illustration. While Jesus was reclining at the table of Simon the Leper, a woman poured a jar of very costly perfume on Jesus' head. Seen as wasteful by the disciples, Jesus responded: "The poor you will always have with you, but you will not always have me."[3]

Both of these women had some similarities—they lived in the home of men named Simon, for instance. Yet while their stories are different, the biggest thing they had in common was that what they did, in essence, was to honour Jesus.

In the Luke account, the woman washed Jesus' feet; a custom of the day that signified welcome and respect, not to mention hygiene! In Jewish custom, it was an insult for a person to enter a home without someone washing their dusty feet. So it was in this case that Jesus was reclined at Simon the Pharisee's table, with dirty feet. This woman honoured Jesus while the Pharisee dishonoured Him by failing to attend to Him appropriately.

The Pharisee questioned the appropriateness of Jesus allowing this, if He indeed knew who was washing his feet—"the kind of woman" she was. Yet the woman had only come to see Jesus and while there, when confronted with this act of dishonour, was moved to action at the risk of her own embarrassment and ridicule. However, Jesus not only received this woman and her gift (an act of personal sacrifice for her), but afterward forgave her sins, which were many. She had not come for this, but left a changed woman as a result of her selfless act of honour.

In the Matthew account, the act of honour was with expensive perfume. Curious that even some of the disciples thought this act extravagant and excessive because the perfume was very costly. Truly this woman was stunning. Without realizing it, she had anointed Jesus for His death and burial. When Judas betrayed Jesus, He would have smelled and remembered her gift. In the garden of Gethsemane, as Jesus sweat drops of blood, He would still be able to smell her offering on His body. Through the trials in the courts of Pilate and Herod's house and through the beating, through the sting of each lash of the whip, the fragrance of her offering remained. Even as Jesus was on the cross dying, the aroma of her sacrifice would also have hung in the air.

Two important things about honour stand out from this. First, Jesus told the woman in the Matthew account that what she did would be remembered for generations: *every sacrifice, every offering, every person in need we help is remembered by God as memorials of honour.* Second, we honour by honouring the giver, as Jesus honoured that woman: *the depth to which we honour is revealed by the degree to which we give.*

THE FOUNDATION OF HONOUR

When a gift is given, we expect the recipient to say thank you. Have you ever given a gift, or something of value to someone and they didn't thank you for it? The Bible tells the story of ten lepers who were healed by Jesus, but only one of those ten actually came back to honour the One who had healed him by saying "thank You." Only one sought a relationship with the Giver and was the only one of the ten who was made completely whole as a result.[4]

The question is asked in Malachi 3:8, how can a man cheat or dishonour God? God's response is that He is cheated or dishonoured when we do not give what is due. Honour is not only shown in the giving of finances or our thanks, but also in giving our talents and time.

A wedding anniversary is an example of this. A wife actually likes it when her husband has planned to acknowledge and celebrate that special day by taking time and effort to work something out, a reservation in a nice restaurant perhaps. If he decides on his own to buy her flowers and goes to a florist and personally selects the flowers and the arrangement, that says so much to her about how he feels. Something planned well, a sacrifice of time and effort shows honour for the relationship.

Put simply, it is not the act of giving the gift, it is the act of giving ourselves, because giving is a demonstration honour.

The act of honour actually is a God-quality and when we honour both God and people, we bring God into each person's life by reason of example.

We are Christ's ambassadors; God is making his appeal through us. We speak for Christ.[5]

How do we treat a stranger, our neighbor, our co-workers—anyone who comes across our path?

Show proper respect to everyone: Love the brotherhood of believers, fear God, honour the king [or those in authority].[6]

In fact, the Bible teaches us to honour one another:

Love must be sincere. Hate what is evil; cling to what is good. Be devoted to one another in brotherly love. *Honour one another above yourselves.*[7]

What does this mean on a practical, day-to-day level? It comes right down to our heart because *honour is an attitude of the heart*. It is much more about that than who we should honour or even why we should honour. Although these also are important elements, the foundation is our heart attitude, beginning with honouring God.

Before David was king and although he'd been anointed by the prophet Samuel as such, he refused to take matters into his own hands in order to bring about his ascension to the throne. When the opportunity came, David refused to harm King Saul who was murderously intent on David's demise. David declared to Saul, "I will never harm the king—he is the LORD'S anointed one,"[8] even though his own men were urging him to kill Saul. David understood honour and chose to honour God by trusting Him. David would not lower himself to become another king like Saul, dishonouring the office, but trusted God to exalt him as king according to His divine plan in His divine timing.

Think about Joseph in the New Testament. When he was about to take Mary as his wife, he discovered that she was pregnant (and not by him!). Joseph acted honourably toward Mary by deciding to quietly break off his engagement to her because by law, her punishment was death. Look at how God responded to him.

As [Joseph] considered this, an angel of the Lord appeared to him in a dream. "Joseph, son of David," the angel said, "do not be afraid to take Mary as your wife. For the child within her was conceived by the Holy Spirit."[9]

This story reveals Joseph's heart attitude; he was a man of honour.

The attitude of honour is what's most important—how we honour and who we honour rather than a list of who deserves our honour. What matters is what happens in our heart when we make the decision to either give honour or withhold it. And that is dependent on an initial life-changing decision we must make: to have the right heart attitude is to yield our lives to Christ and receive salvation, living a life of devotion, making our daily decisions from that place "in Christ."[10]

That is the foundation[11] of honour, for out from this comes the heart desire to please God, to honour Him in the way we live and conduct our lives. The extent to which this is true and the overflow of it is evident by the way we regard and treat others: *we will love and value what God loves and values in proportion to our relationship and submission to Him.* As the following parable told by Jesus reveals, that involves understanding God's heart.

UNDERSTANDING THE FATHER'S HEART

At the beginning of this book we talked about how some grown children demand that their parents given them "what is owed" them before the parents die. A familiar story in the Bible reflects that lack of understanding on the children's part. The parable of the Prodigal Son is well-known. The father had two sons; both were wrong and neither really understood their father's heart toward them. The younger son's lack of understanding showed in what he told his father; so did his lack of honour for his dad:

"I want my share of your estate now before you die." So his father agreed to divide his wealth between his sons. A few days later this younger son packed all his belongings and moved to a distant land.

Little did that boy know what was in store for him because of not knowing his father's heart and dishonouring him.

There he wasted all his money in wild living. About the time his money ran out, a great famine swept over the land, and he began to starve. He persuaded a local farmer to hire him, and the man sent him into his fields to feed the pigs. The young man became so hungry that even the pods he was feeding the pigs looked good to him. But no one gave him anything. When he finally came to his senses, he said to himself, "At home even the hired servants have food enough to spare, and here I am dying of hunger! I will go home to my father and say, 'Father, I have sinned against both heaven and you, and I am no longer worthy of being called your son. Please take me on as a hired servant.'"

When that young man returned home, the depth of his father's heart was revealed in his reaction to the son.

So he returned home to his father. And while he was still a long way off, his father saw him coming. Filled with love and compassion, he ran to his son, embraced him, and kissed him. His son said to him, "Father, I have sinned against both heaven and you, and I am no longer worthy of being called your son." But his father said to the servants, "Quick! Bring the finest robe in the house and put it on him. Get a ring for his finger and sandals for his feet. And kill the calf we have been fattening. We must celebrate with a feast, for this son of mine was dead and has now returned to life. He was lost, but now he is found." So the party began.

Now, you'd think the elder son would be as overjoyed as the father at the younger son's return. In the next passage, however, we see just the opposite.

Meanwhile, the older son was in the fields working. When he returned home, he heard music and dancing in the house, and he asked one of the servants what was going on. "Your brother is back," he was told, "and your father has killed the fattened calf. We are celebrating because of his safe return."

The older brother was angry and wouldn't go in. His father came out and begged him, but he replied, "All these years I've slaved for you and never once refused to do a single thing you told me to. And in all that time you never gave me even one young goat for a feast with my friends. Yet when this son of yours comes back after squandering your money on prostitutes, you celebrate by killing the fattened calf!"

His father said to him, "Look, dear son, you have always stayed by me, and everything I have is yours. We had to celebrate this happy day. For your brother was dead and has come back to life! He was lost, but now he is found!"[12]

The elder son was proud, arrogant, envious and jealous. He believed he was in the right—that his behavior was justified and despite the fact that he was always with his dad, he didn't really know his father's heart. To this son, his hard work and constant presence was honouring of his father and so he couldn't fathom his father's unconditional love and acceptance of his younger, wayward brother. Consequently he was unforgiving, proud and separated himself from both of them. He thought he was behaving honourably, but he wasn't.

What this son failed to realize is what a lot of Christians don't know today—that his father understood things he did not.

The father in this parable understood that the young son was lost but had returned home. This younger son demanded his inheritance because he felt it was rightfully due to him and so he called upon his father to surrender it. He then proceeded to waste his inheritance on riotous living despite his father's goodness. It is so very sad that he couldn't see the end of the road he was taking.

How many people today run from God and can't see the end of the road they're on because they don't know that their Father in heaven is good and they don't know His heart? Jesus said to His disciples one time, "Have I been with you so long, and yet you have not known Me?"[13] Some Christians have been in Christ for years and may even know a great deal about Him; yet they do not know Him despite all the things they have seen Him do. So they settle for less, to just get by or survive until they go to heaven; but Jesus said:

> The thief comes only to steal and kill and destroy; I have come that they may have life, and have it to the full.[14]

God has given us abundant life. According to 2 Peter 1:3, He "has given us everything we need for living a godly life." That verse goes on to tell us how we can get this: "We have received all of this by coming to *know him*." Interestingly it took going through severe hardship and reaching the end of his rope for the younger son in the Luke 15 parable to truly know and honour his father. How did that come about?

It wasn't until the Prodigal Son came to the end of his money and was in desperate need that he realized how honourable and good his father was. It dawned on him that his father's servants were treated far better than he was at that moment—his father was honourable and generous, looking after the welfare of those in his service.

Yet even at that point the younger son was not aware of his father's love or his worth until he humbled himself, admitted his error and in so doing was able to experience his father's acceptance and forgiveness. Look again at the son's words when he returned home:

I am no longer worthy of being called your son.[15]

What made that son believe he was worthy before he left? When we are family, we are family. The father's depth of love was not based on his son's worthiness. In Christ we are not accepted because of our worthiness, but because of His grace. The father was saying in effect, "You are my son, no matter what you have done. It's not about what you deserve, it's about the fact that you have always been my son and *will* always be my son." What great love! How tragic that his son had to go through all that suffering before he realized what it truly is to be a son.

Although close to their father, neither son knew his heart. Do you know the heart of your heavenly Father? Knowing His heart is the key to everything.

We know how much God loves us, and we have put our trust in Him. God is love, and all who live in love live in God, and God lives in them. And as we live in God, our love grows more perfect.[16]

Remember, the Bible says that if we say we love God but hate our brother or sister (literally and in the Lord), then we are a liar: "for if we don't love people we can see, how can we love God, whom we have not seen?"[17] That means these two elements are inseparable, indivisible. You cannot have one without the other. So if you and I love God, then we will demonstrate that in our love for others. When we love, we give. Giving is an act of honour.

GIVING HONOUR

How do we honour? One act for men is to lead the way in how they honour their wives, kids and others. In fact, it is scriptural:

In the same way, you husbands must give honour to your wives. Treat your wife with understanding as you live together. She may be weaker than you are, but she is your equal partner in God's gift of new life. Treat her as you should so your prayers will not be hindered.[18]

Other ways to honour can be: honour your word, honour those in authority over you, honour your teachers, honour your business partner or boss, honour your spouse, your marriage vows, and on and on. Here are some more:

- Avoid criticism.

- Pray for others always.

- Show gratitude. Say, "thank you." Send a note of blessing and encouragement.

- Avoid gossip—reject it, stay away from it.[19] Always respond with something positive to something negative and if the person won't change the subject, then just walk away.

- Offer to meet a need. Offer to help.

- Give, expecting nothing in return.

- Serve. Offer to give your time to help others. Serve in your church, your school, your community.

- Remember people, important events, remember dates that are important. Some things should never be forgotten; work to remember.

These principles of honour can be applied to your loved ones, mentors, friends—to all you come in contact with daily. In addition, remember:

- Honour one another.

- Honour your word; don't take it lightly. Let your yes be yes and your no be no.

- Honour your leaders and teachers.

- Honour your marriage—don't take it lightly. Don't take the man or woman that God gave you lightly.

- Don't take anything lightly that God has given you in life.

- Honour will always cost you something, but it will always be worth it. Honour will always be accompanied with sacrifice, but there is always reward with it.

- Honour God above the fear of man. Sometimes people are afraid of what others will say about them, but honour God above everything; above all else.

- Practice the golden rule: treat everyone with honour; develop a heart attitude to honour others. Remember, the Bible says that whenever you treat others with kindness it is literally as though you were doing the same for God himself.[21]

These are important and practical things we can do to give honour and yet in reality, honour is not found in a list; it is found in the heart. It is the attitude of a servant, it's humility, it's the lifting up of others around you—even when it costs you, when it is a sacrifice—just because it is the right thing to do. Honour is a biblical principle and the principle is this: whatever you honour you add to your life. It is the principle of sowing and reaping.[22] So choose wisely God's way—to honour. What you honour you give value to and attract to yourself.

ENDNOTES

[1]*Merriam-Webster Online Dictionary*, available from http://www. merriam-webster.com/dictionary/honour, S.V. "honour."

[2]Deuteronomy 30:19.

[3]Proverbs 13:22 NKJV.

[4]Hebrews 9:26; 10:12.

[5]Luke 22:19.

[6]Deuteronomy 5:16 NKJV.

[7]Matthew 25:40; 10:42.

Chapter 1

[1]Exodus 20:12; 1 Timothy 2:1–2.

[2]2 Timothy 4:8.

[3]2 Corinthians 6:14–18.

[4]Based on information from Brown, Driver, Briggs and Gesenius, *The Old Testament Hebrew Lexicon*, "Hebrew Lexicon entry for Kabad," available from http://www.studylight.org/lex/heb/view. cgi?number=3513.

[5]AMP.

[6]ESV.

[7]Proverbs 11:16 KJV.

[8]*Vine's Complete Expository Dictionary of Old and New Testament Words* (Nashville, TN: Thomas Nelson, Inc.; Bath, England: W. E. Vine, 1996), S.V. "To Honour."

[9]Brown, Driver, Briggs and Gesenius, "Hebrew Lexicon entry for Kabed," available from http://www.studylight.org/lex/heb/view.

cgi?number=3515, S.V. "heavy," Exodus 17:12.

[10]KJV.

[11]Exodus 17:11.

[12]Romans 16:16; 1 Corinthians 16:20; 2 Corinthians 13:12; 1 Thessalonians 5:26.

[13]Exodus 20:12.

[14]Matthew 22:3,39.

[15]John 15:12.

[16]NIV.

[17]NASB.

[18]John 15:13.

Chapter 2

[1]Based on information from the article *U.S. Decorated Veteran, 90, Fights to Raise Flag in His Yard,* FOXnews.com and the Associated Press,December 3, 2009, available from http://www.foxnews.com/us/2009/12/03/decorated-veteran-fights-raise-flag-yard.

[2]Genesis 8:22.

[3]Genesis 3.

[4]Genesis 9:15–17.

[5]Exodus 12:3–10.

[6]John 1:29; Hebrews 9:26.

[7]Exodus 12:13.

[8]1 John 1:9.

[9]2 Corinthians 5:21.

[10]Just as the Israelites applied the lamb's blood to the doorposts of their houses, "we apply the promises to ourselves and the benefits of the blood of Christ laid up in them. [The blood] was to be sprinkled upon the door-posts, denoting the open profession we are to make of

faith in Christ, and obedience to him, as those that are not ashamed to own our dependence upon him." *Matthew Henry's Commentary on the Whole Bible*, available from http://www.biblestudytools.com/commentaries/matthew-henry-complete/exodus/12.html, S.V. Exodus 12:1–20.

[11]Exodus 13:1–5.

[12]Shmuel Ross, "Passover, Celebration of the Exodus," available from http://www.infoplease.com/spot/passover.html; Also, Thayer and Smith, *The New Testament Greek Lexicon*, "Greek Lexicon entry for Pascha," available from http://www.studylight.org/lex/grk/view.cgi?number=3957, S.V. "Passover," Mark 14:1.

[13]Deuteronomy 4:10.

[14]Luke 22:19.

Chapter 3

[1]Based on information from *The Adam Clarke Commentary*, available from http://studylight.org/com/acc/viewcgi?book=ho&chapter=013, S.V. "Verse 6," Hosea 13:6.

[2]1 Peter 5:8.

[3]James 4:8.

[4]Psalm 16:11 KJV.

[5]Based on information from Brown, Driver, Briggs and Gesenius, *The KJV Old Testament Hebrew Lexicon*, "Hebrew Lexicon entry for Zeker," available from http://www.biblestudytools.com/lexicons/hebrew/kjv/zeker.html, S.V. "memorial," Exodus 3:15; also *The New Testament Greek Lexicon*, Strong's #3422 and 3421, available from http://www.studylight.org/lex/grk/view.cgi?number=3422, S.V. "memorial"; also from *The Old Testament Hebrew Lexicon*, Strong's #2146, available from http://www.studylight.org/lex/grk/view.cgi?number=3422, S.V. "memorial," Joshua 4:7.

[6]Definition taken from *Merriam-Webster Online Dictionary*, available from http://www.merriam-webster.com/dictionary/memorial, S.V. "memorial."

[7]Joshua 1–3, 6–9.

[8]Revelation 5:8.

[9]Revelation 5:5; John 1:36; 1 Peter 1:19; Revelation 5: 8.

[10]Revelation 5:8.

[11]Revelation 8:3.

[12]Acts 10:1–4. KJ21

[13]John 5:44.

Chapter 4

[1]A fourth soldier who served in the Vietnam War was interred in this tomb until the remains of the Vietnam Unknown were exhumed May 14, 1998. Based on mitochondrial DNA testing, DoD scientists identified the remains as those of Air Force 1st Lt. Michael Joseph Blassie, who was shot down near An Loc, Vietnam, in 1972. It has been decided that the crypt that contained the remains of the Vietnam Unknown will remain vacant. This information was taken from http://www.arlingtoncemetery.mil/visitor_information/tomb_of_the_unknowns.html, S.V. "The Unknown of Vietnam."

[2]Information taken from http://en.wikipedia.org/Guard_Mounting#United_States, S.V. "United States."

[3]John Rutherford, producer, NBC News, "4-Hour Shoeshine Honours Nation's Military," available from http://fieldnotes.msnbc.msn.com/_news/2008/11/11/4377176-4-hour-shoeshine-honours-nations-military.

[4]Material taken from an article that ran in a Georgia newspaper called *The Weekly*, available from http://www.theweekly.com/news/2004/May/30/Tomb.html, S.V. "Tomb of the Unknown

Soldier; They Disobeyed the Order."

[5]Philippians 1:21 NASB.

[6]Luke 22:42 KJV.

[7]Luke 22:19 KJV.

[8]1 Timothy 6:12; 2 Timothy4:7.

[9]1 Corinthians 6:19–20; 7:23.

[10]Exodus 31:2 CEV.

[11]Exodus 31:2–5.

[12]Exodus 20:4–6.

[13]Hebrews 9:7, 25.

[14]Ecclesiastes 9:13–15.

[15]1 Timothy 5:17 NKJV.

[16]1 Timothy 5:17.

[17]Based on information from Thayer and Smith, The KJV New Testament Greek Lexicon, "Greek Lexicon entry for Time," available from http://www.biblestudytools.com/lexicons/greek/kjv/time.html, S.V. "honour," 1 Timothy 5:17.

[18]Matthew 25:14–30.

[19]Matthew 25:21.

[20]James 3:1

[21]Davin Granroth, "Clergy Statistics and Resources," July 21, 2008, available from http://www.yearofjubilee.org/2008/07/clergy-statistics-and-resources.

[22]Romans 12:5; 1 Corinthians 12:2,27.

[23]Matthew 26:31 KJV.

Chapter 5

[1]Ephesians 2:9 AMP

[2]The Presidential Medal of Freedom is the highest civilian award in the United States and is bestowed by the President of the United

States. It is designed to recognize individuals who have made "an especially meritorious contribution to the security or national interests of the United States, world peace, cultural or other significant public or private endeavors." Information is from New World Encyclopedia, "Presidential Medal of Freedom," available from http://www.newworldencyclopedia.org/entry/Presidential_ Medal_of_Freedom.

[3]Quotation available from http://www.homeofheroes.com/moh/ citations_1960_vn/benavidez_roy.html .

[4]On an interesting side note, because of protocol, a soldier always salutes an officer; an officer salutes a higher officer all the way up to the General. The highest rank in any Military is the Commander in Chief. The President is the Commander in Chief; he is the highest ranking officer. The Generals of the ranks salute the President but in the United States, when the President sees the Medal of Honor on the chest of a soldier, even a private, the President will salute him. The commander in Chief expresses honour to that individual because they went beyond the call of duty.

[5]Romans 12:1KJV.

[6]Acts 6:1.

[7]Acts 6:2–6.

[8]Ephesians 2:9 AMP.

[9]Based on information from *Merriam-Webster Online Dictionary*, available from http://www.merriam-webster.com/dictionary/grace, S.V. "grace." Also, Thayer and Smith, "Greek Lexicon entry for Charis," available from http://www.biblestudytools.com/lexicons/ greek/kjv/charis.html, S.V. "grace," Ephesians 2:8.

[10]Isaiah 64:6.

[11]Revelation 5:13.

¹²Ephesians 3:20 NKJV.

¹³1 Peter 5:4; Revelation 3:11 ESV.

¹⁴NKJV.

¹⁵Acts 7:51–54.

¹⁶Acts 7:55–56 NIV.

¹⁷Esther 4:1; 5:1–2 NKJV.

Chapter 6

¹This information was taken from the National Park Service, U.S. Department of Interior, "Vietnam War Veterans Memorial," "Introduction," available from http://www.nps.gov/vive/index.htm.

²Ibid., "Korean War Veterans Memorial," "Introduction," available from http://www.nps.gov/kowa/index.htm.

³Psalm 7:15 CEV.

⁴Quote taken from the article "Jeremy Michael Boorda," available from http://www.arlingtoncemetery.net/borda.htm.

⁵Ecclesiastes 10:12.

⁶*Life Application Study Bible* (Carol Stream, IL: Tyndale House Publishers, Inc., 1988, 1989, 1990, 1991, 2005; Grand Rapids, MI: Zondervan), Esther synopsis at the beginning of the book of Esther, p. 748.

⁷2 Kings 5:14.

⁸2 Kings 5:15–16,20–27.

⁹1 Samuel 18:6–11.

¹⁰Romans 13:7 NKJV.

¹¹1 Corinthians 13:4.

¹²Matthew 20:4.

¹³Matthew 20:11–12.

¹⁴Matthew 20:13–15.

[15]Acts 4:36–37.

[16]Acts 5:1–10.

[17]Acts 4:36.

[18]Based on information from Thayer and Smith, *The New Testament Greek Lexicon,* "Greek Lexicon entry for Ananias," available from <http://www.studylight.org/lex/grk/view.cgi?number=367, S.V. "Ananias."

[19]Eastor, Matthew George. "Entry for Sapphira". *Easton's Bible Dictionary.*

[20]Numbers 13, 14.

[21]Brown, Driver, Briggs and Gesenius, *The KJV Old Testament Hebrew Lexicon,* "Hebrew Lexicon entry for Y@howshuwa`," available from http://www.biblestudytools.com/lexicons/hebrew/kjv/yehowshuwa.html, S.V. "Joshua," Numbers 14:6.

[22]Brown, Driver, Briggs and Gesenius, "Hebrew Lexicon entry for Kaleb," available from http://www.biblestudytools.com/lexicons/hebrew/kjv/kaleb.html, S.V. "Caleb," Numbers 14:6.

[23]Joshua 14:12–14.

[24]All information on the meaning of the names of the spies was taken from *Easton's Bible Dictionary.*

Chapter 7

[1]D.A. Pollock, P. Rhodes, C.A. Boyle, P. Decoufle and D.L. McGee, Center for Environmental Health and Injury Control, Centers for Disease Control, Atlanta, GA, "Estimating the Number of Suicides Among Vietnam Veterans," *The American Journal of Psychiatry* 147, 6 June 1990, 772–776, available from http://www.ncbi.nlm.nih.gov/pubmed/2343923.

[2]Based on information from an article by Paul S. Boyer, "Vietnam Veterans Memorial," *The Oxford Companion to United States*

History, 2001, Encyclopedia.com, available from http://www.
encyclopedia.com/topic/Vietnam_Veterans_Memorial.aspx#3-
10119:VietnamVeteransMemorial-full.

[3]Hebrews 11:6.

[4]Luke18:28–30 MSG.

[5]"I Heart Revolution: With Hearts as One," a documentary concert/
witnessing film featuring the Christian rock group Hillsong United,
directed by Danielle Saleh and Joel Houston, DVD release date
May 18, 2010.

[6]Hebrews 12:2.

[7]2 Corinthians 8:9.

[8]AMP.

[9]Hebrews 11:13–16.

[10]Hebrews 11:4 NKJV.

[11]Genesis 5:24.

[12]Genesis 2:5–6 indicates that it hadn't rained before the Flood.

[13]Hebrews 11:8.

[14]Hebrews 11:24–27; Exodus 2.

[15]Hebrews 11:10 MSG.

[16]Hebrews 11:26.

[17]Quotation by David Livingstone was taken from the *Youth
With a Mission* (YWAM) Web site, available from http://www.
ywamorlando.org/int/int_news.asp, S.V. "About Us."

[18]Matthew 10:5–42; 28:16–20.

[19]1 Timothy 6:15; Revelation 17:14; 19:16.

[20]Matthew 28:18–20.

[21]Based on information from *Albert Barnes Notes on the New
Testament,* available from http://www.studylight.org/com/bnn/view.
cgi?book=mt&chapter=028, S.V. "Verse 19," Matthew 28:19.

[22]Quote by John Stewart Mill available from http://www. quotationspage.com/quote/27169.html.

[23]Matthew 13:38–39; Luke 10:19.

[24]1 Samuel 17:1–3.

[25]1 Samuel 17:8–11.

[26]1 Samuel 17:4–7.

[27]Romans 8:31.

[28]Hebrews 13:6.

[29]1 Samuel 17:25.

[30]1 Samuel 17:45–48.

[31]Genesis 1:26.

[32]Joshua 1:1–2.

[33]Joshua 24:15 NKJV.

[34]Luke18:28–30 MSG.

[35]1 Timothy 6:12.

[36]Ephesians 1:18 NKJV.

[37]Revelation 20:12–15.

[38]Revelation 19:6–9 NIV.

[39]2 Timothy 4:7 KJV.

Chapter 8

[1]Based on information from *Merriam-Webster Online Dictionary,* availablefromhttp://www.merriam-webster.com/dictionary/testudo, S.V. "testudo."

[2]Cassius Dio, *Roman History Book* 49, 30, ed. Loeb Classical Library, ISBN 0674-99091-9, available from http://en.wikipedia.org/wiki/ Testudo_formation, S.V. "Description."

[3]Quote taken from *Wikipedia, the Free Encyclopedia,* available from http://en.wikipedia.org/wiki/Spartan_army, S.V. "Spartan army, Training."

[4]Ephesians 6:11 NKJV.

[5]Ephesians 6:14–18.

[6]Jamieson, Fausset, and Brown, *Commentary Critical and Explanatory on the Whole Bible*, available from http://www.studylight.org/com/ jfb/view.cgi?book=eph&chapter=006, S.V. "14. stand," Ephesians 6:14.

[7]See 1 Samuel 17:39.

[8]Ephesians 6:16 NKJV.

[9]Ecclesiastes 4:9 NKJV.

[10]Deuteronomy 32:30.

[11]Timothy 6:12.

[12]Revelation 2:7,11, 3:12,21 NKJV.

[13]Genesis 46:20; Joshua 1:1–5.

[14]Psalm 78:9.

[15]Revelation 7:4–8.

[16]Psalm 91:15.

[17]Brown, Driver, Briggs and Gesenius, *The KJV Old Testament Hebrew Lexicon*, "Hebrew Lexicon entry for Chalats," available from http://www.biblestudytools.com/lexicons/hebrew/kjv/chalats.html, Strong's #2502, S.V. "deliver," Psalm 91:15.

[18]2 John 1:8.

[19]Numbers 13; 14:1–4.

[20]Matthw 24:14.

[21]Isaiah 40:29–31 NKJV.

[22]Keil and Delitzsch *Commentary on the Old Testament*, available from http://www.godrules.net/library/delitzsch/26delitzsch_a0.htm, S.V. "Genesis to Leviticus, Exodus 19:3–4."

[23]*John Gill's Exposition of the Bible*, available from http://www. biblestudytools.com/commentaries/gills-exposition-of-the-bible/

isaiah-40-31.html, S.V. "they shall mount up with wings as eagles," Isaiah 40:31.

Chapter 9
[1]1 Timothy 1:6.
[2]Ephesians 6:18.
[3]M.G. Easton, *Easton's Illustrated Bible Dictionary* (New York, NY; 2006), 333–334, S.V. "holiness."
[4]Matthew 4:4.
[5]1 Peter 2:2.
[6]John 4:32 KJV.
[7]Quote taken from Wikipedia online encyclopedia, available from http://en.wikipedia.org/wiki/Guthrum, S.V. "Guthrum; Defeat by Alfred."
[8]Academic, *Academic Dictionaries and Encyclopedias*, available from http://en.academic.ru/dic.nsf/enwiki/100869, S.V. "Battle of the Catalaunian Plains—Historical importance Traditional view: The battle was of macrohistorical importance."
[9]Quote taken from Wikipedia online encyclopedia, available from http://en.wikipedia.org/wiki/Battle_of_Trenton, S.V. "The Battle of Trenton—Crossing and March."
[10]Ibid.
[11]Thomas Paine (1732–1799) was one of the greatest writers of the Revolutionary era. This quote is the opening words in the first of a series of pamphlets he wrote known as "The Crisis," first published December 19, 1776; excerpted from *Common Sense and Other Political Writings* (Indianapolis, Indiana: Bobbs-Merrill Educational Publishing, 1953), 55.
[12]Ibid.

[13]Genesis 25:27–34.

[14]Ruth 1:1–2.

[15]Genesis 19:30–37.

[16]Ruth 1:2–18.

[17]Daniel 7:25 NASB.

[18]Proverbs 18:10 NIV.

[19]Isaiah 40:28–31.

[20]Galatians 6:9 NIV.

Chapter 10

[1]Based on information from Wikipedia online encyclopedia, available from http://en.wikipedia.org/wiki/Historical_basis_for_King_Arthur.

[2]Quote taken from *King Arthur and the Knights of the Roundtable*, "Sir Lancelot Du Lac," available from http://www.kingarthursknights.com/knights/launcelot.asp.

[3]Quote taken from " Sir Lancelot and Queen Guinevere," available from http://www.sir-lancelot.co.uk/Guinevere-Lancelot.htm.

[4]*Merriam-Webster On-line Dictionary*, available from http://www.merriam-webster.com/dictionary/chivalrous, S.V. "chivalrous."

[5]Deuteronomy 28:44.

[6]2 Corinthians 3:2.

[7]Edwin Louis Cole, *Maximized Manhood* (New Kensington, Pennsylvania: Whitaker House, 2001).

[8]AMP.

[9]Philippians 2:9–11.

[10]Genesis 1:26 KJV.

Chapter 11

[1]NKJV.

[2]Luke 6:45.

[3]1 Samuel 16:7.

[4]*Merriam-Webster Online Dictionary*, available from http://www. merriam-webster.com/dictionary/heart, S.V. "heart."

[5]1Timothy 6:12.

[6]Romans 6:23.

[7]Jamison, Fausset, Brown *Commentary Critical and Explanatory on the Whole Bible*, available from   http://www.blueletterbible.org/ commentaries/comm_view.cfm?AuthorID=7&contentID=2748&c ommInfo=6&topic=Daniel, S.V. "3. Beasts."

[8]Daniel 7:1–7.

[9]Matthew 11:2–3.

[10]Daniel 7:8.

[11]Daniel 7:22 NIV.

[12]NKJV.

[13]Daniel 7:9–12 CEV.

[14]Matthew 28:2–4; Revelation 1:17.

[15]Isaiah 6:5 KJV.

[16]Isaiah 6:3; Revelation 4:8.

[17]Daniel 7:25 NIV.

[18]John Gill *Exposition of the Entire Bible*, available from http:// www.studylight.org/com/geb/view.cgi?book=1jo&chapter=004&ve rse=003, S.V. "And this is that [spirit] of antichrist," 1 John 4:3.

[19]Genesis 3:4–5.

[20]Matthew 4:11.

[21]Luke 10:18.

[22]Isaiah 14:13–14 AMP.

[23]Romans 8:11.

[24]Revelation 20:1–3, 7–10.

[25]Joel 2:31; Matthew 24; Revelation 20:12–15.

[26]KJV.

[27]Joshua 1:3,5.

[28]Joshua 12:7–24.

[29]Joshua 1:7, 9,18; 10:25; 17:18.

[30]Ephesians 6:12 NIV.

[31]Ephesians 6:13 NKJV.

[32]1 Corinthians 15:57.

[33]Hebrews 6:10–12.

[34]Galatians 6:9.

Chapter 12

[1]1 Samuel 17:34–36.

[2]Luke 7:47 NIV.

[3]Matthew 26:11 NIV.

[4]Luke 17:11–19.

[5]2 Corinthians 5:20.

[6]1 Peter 2:17 NIV.

[7]Romans12:9–10 NIV.

[8]1 Samuel 24:10.

[9]Matthew 1:20.

[10]2 Timothy 2:10 AMP.

[11]1 Corinthians 3:11.

[12]Luke 15:11–32.

[13]John 14:9.

[14]John 10:10 NIV.

[15]Luke 15:19.

[16]1 John 4:16–17.

[17]1 John 4:20.

[18]1 Peter 3:7.
[19]James 1:26.
[20]Mathew 5:37.
[21]Matthew 25:40; 10:42.
[22]Galatians 6:7.

ABOUT THE AUTHOR

 Robert and his wife Karyn moved to Lima, Peru in 1983 and are settled in for the long haul...you'll often hear them quoting, "long term missions, long term results." They love God's church and have a passion to team up with other churches throughout South America to see them reach their full potential.

Robert Barriger is the founding pastor of Camino de Vida Church in Lima, Peru. Today Camino de Vida is an influential church in Peru and South America. The church is known for their work with orphaned and abandoned children, as well as helping the poor and disabled.

Pastor Robert and Karyn have 2 married children, who serve with them in their work and three beautiful grandchildren.

Prayer of Salvation

God loves you—no matter who you are, no matter what your past. God loves you so much that He gave His one and only begotten Son for you. The Bible tells us that "…whoever believes in him shall not perish but have eternal life" (John 3:16 NIV). Jesus laid down His life and rose again so we could spend eternity with Him in heaven and experience His absolute best on earth. If you would like to receive Jesus into your life, say the following prayer out loud and mean it from your heart.

Heavenly Father, I come to You admitting that I am a sinner. Right now, I choose to turn away from sin, and I ask You to cleanse me of all unrighteousness. I believe that Your Son, Jesus, died on the cross to take away my sins. I also believe that He rose again from the dead so that I might be forgiven of my sins and made righteous through faith in Him. I call upon the name of Jesus Christ to be the Savior and Lord of my life. Jesus, I choose to follow You and ask that You fill me with the power of the Holy Spirit. I declare that right now I am a child of God. I am free from sin and full of the righteousness of God. I am saved in Jesus' name. Amen.

If you prayed this prayer to receive Jesus Christ as your Savior for the first time, please contact us on the Web at **harrisonhouse.com** to receive a free book.

Or you may write to us at

Harrison House
P.O. Box 35035
Tulsa, OK 74153

The Harrison House Vision

Proclaiming the truth and the power

Of the Gospel of Jesus Christ

With excellence;

Challenging Christians to

Live victoriously,

Grow spiritually,

Know God intimately.

Fast. Easy. Convenient.

For the latest Harrison House product information and author news, look no further than your computer. All the details on our powerful, life-changing products are just a click away. New releases, E-mail subscriptions, testimonies, monthly specials—find it all in one place. Visit harrisonhouse.com today!

harrisonhouse